Killings

Folk Justice in
the Upper South

WILLIAM LYNWOOD MONTELL

THE UNIVERSITY PRESS OF KENTUCKY

Scholarly publisher for the Commonwealth,
serving Bellarmine College, Berea College, Centre
College of Kentucky, Eastern Kentucky University,
The Filson Club Historical Society, Georgetown College,
Kentucky Historical Society, Kentucky State University,
Morehead State University, Murray State University,
Northern Kentucky University, Transylvania University,
University of Kentucky, University of Louisville,
and Western Kentucky University.
All rights reserved.

Editorial and Sales Offices: The University Press of Kentucky
663 South Limestone Street, Lexington, Kentucky 40508-4008

03   3   4   5   6

Library of Congress Cataloging-in-Publication Data

Montell, William Lynwood, 1931–
    Killings: folk justice in the Upper South.

    Bibliography: p.
    Includes index.
    1. Homicide—Kentucky—History.   Homicide—Tennessee—
History.   3. Violence—Kentucky—History.   4. Violence—
Tennessee—History.   5. Kentucky—Rural conditions.
6. Tennessee—Rural conditions.   I. Title.
HV6533.K4M66   1986   364.1'523'09768   86-13358
ISBN 0-8131-0824-1

This book is printed on acid-free recycled paper meeting
the requirements of the American National Standard
for Permanence of Paper for Printed Library Materials.

Manufactured in the United States of America

For Barbara

Contents

Acknowledgments

I began field research on this project in August 1978 and continued at regular intervals through April 1985, as my teaching schedule permitted. The bulk of the research was completed by July 1984, at which time I began to organize the materials in preparation for writing. The manuscript was completed during the 1984-85 academic year while I was on sabbatical leave. The Faculty Research Committee of Western Kentucky University provided financial support during the early stages of the project. I wish especially to thank my department head, Carol P. Brown, and dean, Ward Hellstrom, along with my departmental colleagues, Jay Anderson, Cam Collins, Burt Feintuch, and Marilyn White, who encouraged and supported me in many ways. Thanks also to Donald P. Costello, Chairman of the Department of American Studies at the University of Notre Dame, for inviting me to teach as a visiting professor during the spring term of 1985, and to Dean Michael Loux for providing me with full stenographic services and access to the personal computer lab of Notre Dame's College of Arts and Letters.

My debt to the narrators is heaviest of all, for without them there would be no book. They are, in a real sense, coauthors. In what has proved to be the single most difficult decision in my professional career, I have chosen to omit their real names from this published study in order to shield them from any possible embarrassment and harassment. Because of the delicate and sensitive nature of the information they shared with me, I have substituted fictitious designations for all persons and places in the study area and its environs.

The decision not to recognize these local historians by name was made even more difficult by the knowledge that the past is extremely relevant to all of them, and is spoken of only in the most positive terms. There is an uncanny presence of history in most of what they think and say and do. Their constant attribution of information to its source within the community not only validates the accounts in their eyes; it also makes a strong statement that such events were talked about among members of the community across the years, thus helping me to corroborate the accounts.

Certain individuals, not always narrators, were indispensable in other ways to the successful completion of this project. A woman who was for many years a resident of "Brownsville" willingly corresponded with me throughout the project, and read and criticized the manuscript before I changed the names of the people involved. A woman from "Mattis" shared equally valuable memories of that community which she had carefully preserved in her head and in a daily log for more than 60 years. She introduced me to various other persons as well, helped to interview them, advised me on many matters, and corresponded with me on numerous occasions. Also helpful were her son, who took me into the heart of the research area by means of a four-wheel-drive vehicle and assisted my fieldwork; a three-member family from "Lightsboro" who acted as go-betweens in my meetings with new people, hauled me around the countryside in their family pickup, and provided an abundance of friendship, fellowship, and fine food; two former students who introduced me to relevant portions of the study area in "Owenton" County; Captain Barton Duke of the "Northtown," Indiana, police department, who provided valuable information gleaned from the city's old arrest records; two local historians from "Brake" and "Fountain" counties, who furnished me with personal documents pertaining to institutional life and history in their portions of the study area; the "Fountain" County judge executive, who assisted in countless ways; John Dowell, Sharon Celsor, and Drew Beisswenger, who labored diligently and faithfully on this project as my research assistants in the folk studies program at Western Kentucky University; and members of my undergraduate folk studies class during the fall term of 1981, who collectively interviewed five persons. Simultaneous thanks and apologies are due all the local historians across the years whose works were invaluable to me but who, again in the interest of anonymity, cannot be cited formally.

A debt of gratitude to librarians and archivists must be acknowledged, especially those in Western Kentucky University's Folklife Archives (where the tapes and supporting documents recorded or obtained in connection with this project are stored and will be open to the public on January 1, 2025), and in the Kentucky Library, also at Western. Similar credit is due the competent staffs of the Tennessee State Library and Archives, Nashville; the Kentucky Department for Libraries and Archives, Frankfort (especially Tommy Griffin); the Kentucky Historical Society Library, Frankfort (especially Linda Anderson); the Oral History Office and Special Collections at the University of Kentucky, Lexington; the public library in "Jessetown," Tennessee (especially the head librarian); and the public library in "Washington," Kentucky (particularly the head librarian and bookmobile librarian).

The biggest thank you of all goes to Barbara, my wife and research companion. She was with me much of the time in the State Line country where we shared notes at the end of each interview, and often discussed new ideas and theories surrounding the research at the end of the day. She also listened patiently during the writing stage (a noble act indeed, since she was in the process of writing a manuscript of her own), gently prodded when I grew tired, and offered positive criticism of the finished manuscript. To her, this book is dedicated with love and appreciation.

Introduction

During Indiana University's spring term, 1963, visiting professor Carl O. Sauer issued a challenge to a graduate seminar in cultural geography, of which I was a member. His charge to us was to select a small geographical area for study, return to it every 15 years to observe the changes that had taken place, and attempt to explain why they came about. Following this advice, I chose a small portion of the Upper South, mainly because of its proximity to Campbellsville College, where I taught from 1963 to 1969, and to Western Kentucky University, which has served as my academic home base since that time. The bulk of my research and publishing activity has thus largely been focused on this portion of the Upper South.

This time I have chosen to probe more deeply into local history and life by investigating one aspect of the area's culture: namely, homicidal behavior within a smaller geographical area in the region, referred to herein as the State Line country. My intention has been twofold: first, to identify the chief historical and social conditions and the prevailing attitudes and values that engendered and perpetuated rowdy behavior and homicidal activity across the years; second, to determine whether, in the process, the people in the study area created and fostered a culture of violence. The term "homicide" is employed to indicate that the study is concerned with murder and manslaughter which generally resulted from interpersonal (one-on-one) disagreements and altercations. Civil War–related mayhem is touched only for historical context, and feuding will not be addressed here, as family vendettas were rare in this general locality.

The geographical area in which this examination of lethal interpersonal violence takes place is situated astraddle the Kentucky-Tennessee state line, a little east of the midpoint. It is a roughtly rectangular entity that extends for approximately nine miles from north to south and ten miles from east to west. The area is unequally divided by counties that I have designated Brake and Owenton in Kentucky, and Fountain and Trundle in Tennessee. Brake and Trundle contain most of the territory and consequently witnessed most of the killings that took place here.

All together, there are 50 documented homicides between the mid-1880s and 1940, but only six more through 1979. Numerous additional unverified homicides are rumored to have occurred, mainly between 1900 and 1920. While there may be substance to some of these reports, I have chosen to omit them from consideration and base my comments and conclusions on the 50 killings that are verified by court records or substantial oral tradition.

"Killing" is the only term recognized and used within the community for the type of action described here. "Murder" is much too strong, as it connotes a viciousness that was not present and not appropriate, at least in the minds of local residents. Thus, the additional terms I have used—violence, violent behavior, deviant behavior, homicide, homicidal behavior, murder, manslaughter—were chosen, after considerable hesitation, because they are commonly used by social scientists, although not by local narrators.

Population was fairly stable between 1880 and 1940, with an annual average of some 1,225 persons in the study area during the height of homicidal activity there. That figure dropped to approximately 1,000 after 1940. Their ancestors migrated largely from the British Isles during colonial times. Present residents of the study area are exclusively white Protestants, and have been since the 1920s when the last two black families left. Local economy has historically been based mainly on small, marginally productive, single-family farms. Hunting and gathering were extensively engaged in until the 1930s, and moonshining was a standard activity well into the 1950s. Extensive stands of cutover hardwood forests, once the target of large sawmilling ventures, are located in the rugged, almost inaccessible interior of the area. A few persons now work in garment factories and stores in the little county seat towns or in some form of public employment, but there are not enough such jobs to go around, and the effects of low incomes and unemployment are critically felt. Although poor by outside standards—more so now than earlier—these people have witnessed the growth and development of a stable, essentially egalitarian society.

On the surface, the culture of the State Line country resembles what Wolfgang and Ferracuti referred to as a "subculture of violence,"[1] in which violence and aggression are natural responses to threats, insults, and displays of weapons. Specific standards of behavior are learned and passed on by inculcation; thus, the more integrated an individual is into such a subculture, the greater the likelihood that the person will engage in violent behavior. When an act of violence is committed in such a setting, it is done without guilt, for the act is not considered wrong by group standards. In this sense, the offender is not a deviant, but rather a conformist to the social values of the group. While these attributes may appear at first to fit the State Line country, killing here was never done by hardened criminals. And from the insider's perspective, the offenders were generally moral, God-fearing individuals, with full social status within the community. There was, nevertheless, a culture of violence at work in the State Line country. That issue will be addressed in the Conclusion after all the available data have been introduced.

The hypothesis upon which this study rests may be stated as follows: Interpersonal lethal violence was an acceptable way of handling disagreements and tensions among residents of the State Line country. This position, while nothing new to criminologists who study violence mainly in urban settings, raises a series of questions about the specific nature and role of interpersonal violence in a culturally stable rural area. Why

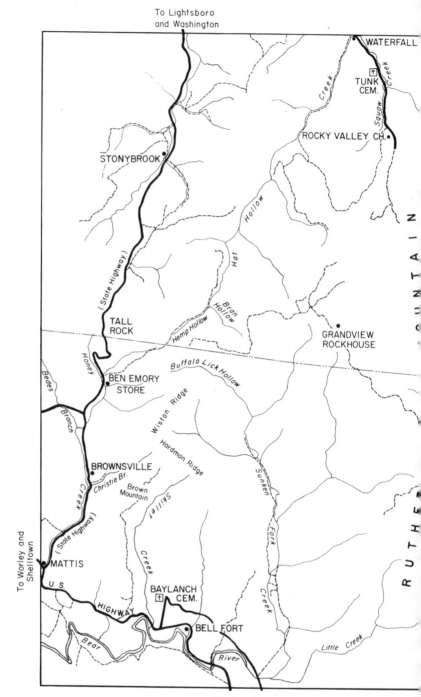

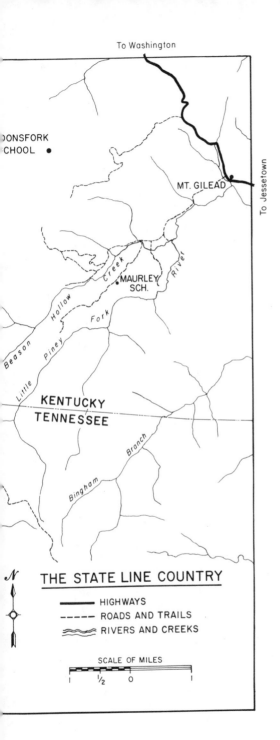

The State Line Country

did members of the community frequently settle disputes and redress grievances by means of homicidal violence rather than through available legal channels? What was the prevailing attitude toward the law and law enforcement officers? To what extent did the victims provoke their attackers, intentionally causing them to suffer grief, anxiety, or anguish through such nonphysical means as obscene or abusive language? To what extent did certain facets of domestic life and culture create tensions that are resolved by fighting and killing? What was the influence of the rugged physical landscape, and its division into smaller political units, on illegal activities? To what extent did making, selling, and consuming moonshine whiskey influence lethal violence? What was the role of tradition in making violence an acceptable form of behavior under a given set of circumstances? To what degree did the Civil War and subsequent industrialization introduced by outsiders influence the character and quality of local life?

In an effort to address these and related issues, I have approached this study of killings ethnographically so as to place the social, cultural, and economic history of the State Line country in holistic perspective. Such a contextual approach allows for the portrayal of lethal violence in its true relation to other elements of the area's culture, rather than in distorted or sensationalized perspective.[2] The use of oral sources makes such an approach possible, as the researcher is compelled to look at killings and their causes through the eyes of insiders. Documentary sources as well as published and unpublished written materials were also gleaned to supplement the oral information and provide as much detail as possible about what happened before, during, and after the homicides.

My introduction to the subject of killings here and the rich narrative tradition surrounding most of these violent episodes came about in 1978 by a rather fortuitous circumstance. I had gone with two residents of Honey Creek (located in Trundle County, Tennessee) to Walnut Ridge (a tiny community situated just over the line in Brake County, Kentucky) to talk with two men and a woman, all of whom were in their late 70s. The woman was the wife of one man and the sister of the other. At that time, I was researching a hanging that had taken place in 1872 in a Tennessee town some 30 miles away. All three of them knew about the hanging and told me as much as they knew. Obtaining the desired information was somewhat difficult, however, as they frequently changed the subject. They were not avoiding the questions; they were just more interested in topics closer home. When the interview was over, one of the men turned to me and suggested, "Why don't you let me and him and Old Claxton down here at the store tell you all about the killings that took place up here on the state line down across the years? We are the only ones left that can set the record straight." The other man nodded agreement.

Three weeks later I went back, still not knowing exactly what lay in store. Although I usually have a prepared set of questions to ask during an interview, this time I had nothing. These people would tell me what they wanted me to know. We chatted a few minutes about incidental things before I set up the tape recorder. The man who had suggested the occasion reached into the top pocket of his overalls and produced a neatly folded piece of paper containing a list of 16 slayings, handwritten by his daughter from his dictation. He handed the paper to me, saying, "You read off the names and I'll tell you what I know about each one."

As I read the list, item by item, he would begin, "Oh, yeah, that was the time that . . ." His brother-in-law and sister contributed details now and again until, finally, the list was exhausted. On the basis of the information gathered during this and subsequent interviews with the three, I went on to record the recollections of numerous other people, who provided additional information about the 16 killings and described the family backgrounds of the parties involved in each deadly altercation. Further, as my contacts with other narrators increased, descriptions of still more killings were added, and the geographical base of the inquiry widened.

Once this topic had been selected for investigation, I began a systematic search of newspaper files and available court records in the four Kentucky and Tennessee counties, hoping to find names, records of indictments, court proceedings, and journalistic accounts of the homicides in order to date the killings; such sources might additionally serve, I thought, to corroborate the oral accounts. To say that this search was less than fruitful would be an understatement. Local weeklies from the early years contained news of sensational slayings and natural disasters from New York to California ("Tied to Maddened Horse, Beautiful Wyoming Girl Dragged to an Awful Death"; "Jealousy Cause of Triple Murder in Oklahoma") but rarely a mention of local homicides. Not until the 1940s did the newspapers make a point of carrying limited coverage of the more sensational happenings in their own vicinity. Even then, news of some killings never appeared in the hometown press because neither the editors nor the county sheriffs were informed with any regularity of these events; the story was often old by the time word of a killing drifted into town. Court records are also scarce, since many of the State Line killings were never dealt with through legal channels; moreover, some records were destroyed by fire in three of the four counties.

To supplement the meager journalistic and legal documentation, then, I turned to other sources of information about the study area. Old highway and topographic maps, along with federal census rolls through 1910, proved helpful in approximating the average number of people in the study area, and who lived where and when. Important also were my numerous visits to family and community cemeteries in quest of birth and death dates. Residents frequently made personal papers and old photographs available to me. Some persons had kept diaries and logs of current happenings and weather conditions for many years, and continue to do so. For example, a woman on Honey Creek and her physician father before her kept daily records that, combined, reach back almost 100 years. In total, this background research provided a beginning data base about social, cultural, and economic facets of the area's history. It also suggested the kinds of topics I should pursue during the interview phase. Once the interviewing began, I asked the same general questions of all the narrators about the area's history, and the same specific questions about each killing. This was done in order to achieve consistency in the responses and to aid in sorting out seeming discrepancies and contradictions.

The questioning began by addressing the noncontroversial facets of area life and gradually progressed toward the theme of violence. For example, the subject of home life afforded the opportunity to eventually inquire as to which parent generally punished a disobedient child. To what extent did punishment cause family disputes? Were there any killings as the result of such disagreements? During the interviews, I typically asked about the safety of homemade toys, the ownership and use of pocketknives and guns, situations in which killing was considered justifiable, instances of victim-precipitated homicides, what the community did in the absence of law enforcement officials, the extent (or lack) of respect for constituted law, and a host of other questions designed to elicit specific information about the killings.

No attempt was made to select narrators on the basis of sex or age. The nature of the research called for interviews with those persons who reportedly knew the most about particular killings: those who had been eyewitnesses to actual events, or had viewed the scene of a crime while the bodies were still present; the children of eyewitnesses; and individuals who learned about the episodes from informed talk within the community. In making initial contacts, I relied on two or three friends in each of the four counties to assist me by answering preliminary questions and going with me (sometimes taking me in their pickups and four-wheel-drive vehicles) to meet prospective narrators for the first time. Ultimately, contacts were made with sheriffs, deputies, revenue agents, physicians, schoolteachers, superintendents and other school administrators, who, though often outsiders, had had direct contact with residents of the study area across the years. The bulk of the interviews, however, were with active and retired farmers, farm wives, tenant farmers, lumbermen, ministers, moon-

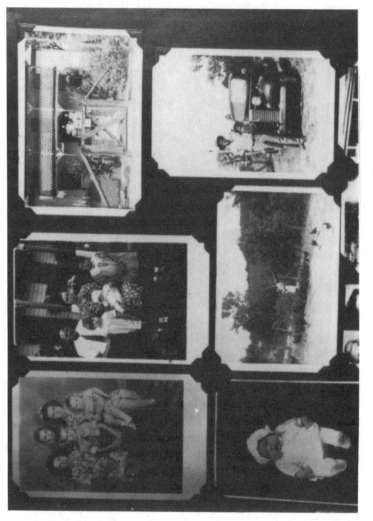

The husband and wife shown here (top center) willingly shared information and friendship to assist the author. These photos are from a family album of the mid-1930s.

shiners, and merchants who lived within the area itself. All together, I obtained information from 60 people and tape-recorded interviews with 39 of them.

The narrators I sought out willingly shared their memories and confidences with me (only one person was uncooperative, answering my questions evasively and refusing to allow me to tape-record or take notes). In addition to their personal recollections of killings, they provided information in the form of oral traditional history: that is, accounts of earlier killings told to them by older residents who had witnessed the events themselves or had, in turn, heard about them from members of previous generations. These rich conversations and narratives are valuable cultural documents that often implicitly explain what and how residents felt about themselves. The existence of such a vigorous repertoire of oral narratives indicates the continuing significance of lethal interpersonal violence as a topic of historical interest among area residents, both past and present. The information narrators shared with me not only reported what happened during particular violent incidents, but often shed light on the value judgments people exercised when weighing the motives for violence against the consequences.

I conducted numerous follow-up interviews, using both tape recorder and note pad, in order to obtain new information and to seek clarification and verification of items previously recorded. Copious field notes were written as well, as soon as possible after each interview. I also relied on telephone calls and correspondence, and sent questionnaires to selected persons.[3] If, for example, I needed additional names and details in the Honey Creek locality, I would dispatch an identical questionnaire requesting specific information to three or four individuals chosen for their presumed knowledge and their willingness to share information in this manner. Persons in Waterfall would receive a similar instrument but with questions relevant to that geographical area only. Details surrounding each homicide were thus verified by several narrators independently.

Not once did the narrators themselves request the deletion or alteration of names and details. They exhibited no desire to hide or camouflage the facts; on the contrary, they manifested a genuine interest in accuracy. Toward that end, I asked one person with intimate knowledge of numerous homicides (by virtue of immediate family involvements) to read the entire finished manuscript. After completing the task, she wrote me: "I don't find anything to change. Only the real names. There's a lot of grandchildren and great-grandchildren of so many of those mentioned, and they would probably object and try to cause trouble."

I am extremely fortunate to have gained entry to the memories of this person and so many others. To them, a local killing was, next to sex and illegitimacy, the most hushed of topics and was typically spoken about only within the immediate community. Superficial details might be shared with outsiders, but subjective thoughts and attitudes toward these events were exclusive to an esoteric audience. I am fully aware that some narrators likely withheld information from me; nonetheless, I believe that, after personally visiting in many homes and attending local functions over a six-year period, I came to be viewed by area residents as a trusted friend.

Such trust and confidence are priceless assets to researchers in the field. For this reason, I feel compelled to shield the identities of those persons who assisted me from public scrutiny and possible condemnation by friends and neighbors. Against the personal wishes of some of the narrators, who felt that the revelation of true identities would not matter, I have changed the names of the killers and victims in every instance, as well as those of all the other State Line residents who appear in the narrative. I was careful to see that all persons with the same surnames in real life were given the same fictitious surnames in the book, and the same is true for first names. Any resemblance between the real names and the pseudonyms is purely coincidental. County and other place names throughout the vicinity have also been altered, as there is no need to subject current residents to possible embarrassment by carrying their community's homicidal reputation to geographical areas where it was heretofore unknown. I hope that even the most vociferous critics of this practice will see from the following pages that my reasons for using psuedonyms are justifiable.[4]

The subject matter in this book falls into four fairly well-defined time periods, each treated in a separate chapter. Chapter 1 looks briefly at early settlement and the environmental influences on nineteenth-century life. It focuses on the rather drastic change in local culture brought about by guerrilla warfare during and after the Civil War, and by the federal tax placed on distilled whiskey after 1873. The killings that occurred between 1865 and 1890 are described against this background of war-related animosities and threats against the personal domains of the moonshiners. Chapter 2 deals with the economically self-sufficient years between 1890 and 1915. This period, though marked by violence, was locally characterized by positive social interaction among the residents, economic self-sufficiency, and overall cultural stability. Much of what was good and seemingly unalterable ended with the coming of large commercial sawmills. That facet of local life, roughly covering the years between the two world wars, is dealt with in Chapter 3. Moonshining and farming are also considered in this chapter as the two chief economic activities that, in essence, worked against sawmilling in ensure a stable quality of life. Chapter 4 contains descriptions of the killings that occurred during that period and probes reasons for the multiplicity of homicides that marked it. Chapter 5 looks at the State Line country since World War II, when outmigration to midwestern agricultural and industrial centers became common, probably accounting for the sudden decline in moonshining and homicidal activities. An analysis of local migrants to one city in Indiana, is presented as a case in point. Finally, the Conclusion analyzes the features of the killings in the study area within a historical and cultural context.

Perhaps the results of this intensive investigation into the history of killings in a small geographical area of the Upper

South will help to alleviate the general informational void
about southern homicides noted by Harries, who wrote, "Our
absolute ignorance of the sources of high southern homicide
rates is an outstanding example of the lack of national commitment with respect to various critical social issues."[5] In a similar vein, Bankston and Allen have suggested the strong
possibility of the existence of southern subregions possessing
violent traditions.[6] They noted that most killings in the South
have been viewed only statistically in comparing southern
homicides with those of other regions; there has been little
attempt to separate such events into rural and urban, race, sex,
and working-class categories. These scholars stressed the need
for specific research designed to identify "values associated
with the possession and carrying of lethal weapons and, especially, the willingness to use them."[7] They apparently believe, as I do, that most of the social scientists who have written
about "southern violence" have done so as if there were a
uniform and consistent pattern of behavior from Richmond to
Houston, from Louisville to Miami. Such a view totally ig-
nores cultural differences brought about by various environmental, social, economic, and historical factors.

It is my position that scholars should not make broad pro-
nouncements regarding the question of southern violence
without first seeking to understand its origins and nature in
specific southern regions.[8] This study proposes to address that
void by investigating homicidal activity across the years in one
small area of the Upper South.

Killings

1

In the Beginning

THE STATE LINE country is shared by two states and four counties—two of them in each state. The area is characterized by rocky hills, steep bluffs, sharp ridges, and narrow valleys. In some instances, prominent ridges may rise 500 to 1,200 feet above the valley floors, while pressing closely against the narrow strips of fertile bottomlands at their base; many other ridges are overly stingy and leave no room for patches of tobacco and corn. The central portion of the area contains a combination of all these physical features, but its rugged and nearly inaccessible terrain explains why local people refer to it as Rutherford Mountain. This upland interior is drained by two small nonnavigable rivers; the Little Piney Fork in Kentucky and the Bear in Tennessee. Both rivers have carved deep channels in some places; their walls consist of precipitous cliffs more than 25 feet high throughout the region, and more than 150 feet in the Little Piney Fork country. An observer standing in the stream channel is dwarfed by the magnificent ridges that loom an additional 1,000 feet or so above the sheer faces of the cliffs. The tributary waters that flow from the center of the mountainous area have laid the entire upland portion open in the manner of a fan having many ribs, and have rendered it useless for agricultural pursuits. Regardless of the compass direction of their individual flow, however, the waters from all of these courses eventually wind up in the Rutherford River, a larger stream that loops around the area and drains it from the north and west.

In spite of the physical limitations of the land, early State Line families were not culturally isolated in the fullest sense of

Looking eastward from Rutherford Mountain over the headwaters of Little Piney Fork River

the word, and most certainly not from their own perspective.[1] In a time when travel throughout the Upper South was accomplished on foot, by animal, or horsedrawn carriage, local people seldom thought about their isolation. While terrain and distance were limiting factors, the early settlers were not totally out of touch with the outside, as illustrated by the presence of a horse-racing track during the earliest decades of the nineteenth century at Maurleysville, a nearby community on the Little Piney Fork;[2] the establishment of the Washingtonian Temperance Society in the Bear River Valley in 1845, very soon after the national temperance movement began; and the formation of a Masonic lodge there before 1850.[3]

The pioneers who settled the State Line country did so without the benefit of a major road any closer than approximately 40 miles, according to a "Map of the State of Kentucky with the Adjoining Territories" published in 1794, and "A Map of the Tennessee [sic] Government" issued in London in 1795.

Roads and trails within the area were located along the crests of ridges and in creek beds wherever possible, so that they would not compete with the plow for available farmland along the stream courses. Like other unimproved rural roads in the Upper South, these were treacherous and muddy, impassable during the winter months. Maintenance of the roads that connected families with each other and provided limited access to the county seat towns was the job of the people who used them. Every ablebodied man was expected to donate six days of labor each year toward this end, or three days if he also furnished a team and wagon for hauling dirt and gravel. Crushed stone was not used in local road construction until the 1930s, and hard-surfaced roads are still scarce.

Today, a blacktop road follows the course of an old wagon road from Washington, Kentucky, to a U.S. highway at Mattis, Tennessee, by way of Lightsboro, Stonybrook, Tall Rock, and Brownsville (see the accompanying map). A dead-end finger of this road begins at Lightsboro, four miles north of the state line, and runs along the upper reaches of Squaw Creek before dying at the base of Rutherford Mountain, one mile from Tennessee. Dirt roads, carved out in pioneer times and now suited only to off-road vehicles, branch off all along the four-mile course, trail across the interior of Rutherford Mountain, and emerge at Mt. Gilead, where a second blacktop artery from Washington was built after World War II. Like adjacent roads in Kentucky, those in Tennessee that branch off the U.S. highway and dart into the Bear River Valley become virtually nonexistent as they trail northward into the interior of Rutherford Mountain, where a dozen or so families—the Talbots, Nesbitts, Panningses, Baylanches, and Parrigans, among others—lived until the 1930s. In 1915, a date that coincides with their occupation of the mountain, a geologist described that locality and its immediate environs as being "more nearly a wilderness in the true sense of the word than any equaled size area east of the Mississippi today."[4]

A fruitless search of the 1910 federal census schedules for certain Rutherford Mountain families in Brake and Trundle counties illustrates both the self-imposed seclusion of their habitations and the inadequacy of the census enumeration system. The census workers either did not want to penetrate the isolated and virtually inaccessible terrain or were unaware that people lived there at all. Yet some families were indeed on Rutherford Mountain at the time, as I talked with a man who resided in the interior at Grandview Rock House as a child and who remembered four other households within shouting distance of each other. Another narrator, who began teaching school 20 years later at Coonsfork (located on the same mountain system between Squaw Creek and Little Piney Fork) described the trail leading to the school in 1930 as "too narrow for a mule to walk on." He then related this humorous anecdote about the absence of roads in the area:

Used to when people lived back there and wanted to come to Washington, they had to go through Tennessee and up through Worley to get to Washington. I saw Howard one day and I said, "Howard, how did you get here?"
   He said, "Come through Georgia!" [laughter]
   It was 60 to 75 miles around.

The families who settled the State Line country in the early to mid-1800s were of the same stock that populated other parts of the Upper South. The 1850 census indicates that in both states they were mainly of American birth and white American parentage, largely from Virginia, North Carolina, and South Carolina. Also, many Tennesseans had been born in Kentucky and numerous Kentuckians were native to Tennessee.[5]
   Revolutionary War veterans or their heirs dominated the earliest settlement thrust between 1800 and 1810. Revolutionary ancestry was so common here that a political orator once referred to a local Kentucky audience as "sons and daughters of the American Revolution."[6] By the time a treaty between the United States and the Cherokees in 1805 opened most of the land in the State Line country to settlers, some were already there (in violation of the earlier Tatewell Treaty of 1785, which had established a line between Indian lands and those set aside

as a military reservation for soldiers of the Revolution), and were pushing against the headwalls of the valleys as they penetrated this heretofore uncharted area. By mid-nineteenth century, they or their progeny had settled all of the valley land that afforded agricultural potential, as well as portions of Rutherford Mountain on both sides of the state line. Included among the names of the pioneer families in the State Line country were most of those later involved in the violence described in this study: Talbot, Black, Tunk, Beardly, Christie, Plinkett, Lyons, Parrigan, Hardcastle, Hill, Boyer, Langness, Bowles, Bowlings, Merton, Hutton, Bede, Bead,[7] Tripps, North, Baylanch, and Billings. Soon to come were the Goins, Coffelt, Faris, Nesbitt, Staton, and Tarter families.

Demographically, the study area consists mainly of five populated valleys, each of which is drained by a river or fairly large creek. These are, along with a listing of some of the places found in each, the Bear River Valley (Bell Fort), and Honey Creek (Brownsville, Mattis) in Tennessee; and Squaw Creek (Rocky Valley, Waterfall), Bingham Branch (Bingham), and Little Piney Fork River (Maurley, Mt. Gilead) in Kentucky. The Bear and Little Piney Fork river valleys historically supported heavier farming populations than the other three. Rutherford Mountain, which is common to all five valleys, was sparsely populated across the years except for the period 1915-35 when logging, sawmilling, and—to a lesser extent—oil-drilling operations attracted some local people to the area. Together, these demographic centers had a total population that averaged 1,225 persons for each census period between the years 1890 and 1940, with never less than 1,095 nor more than 1,330. Because of outmigration between 1940 and 1970, the average figure for those years was approximately 1,035.

Although the two largest river valleys supported farming on a sizable scale across the years, most of the families in the area were sustained by subsistence agriculture and by hunting, fishing, gathering, and moonshining activities. Those persons who populated Rutherford Mountain proper could do little better than eke out a living on the thin, rocky, infertile soils;

they did not attempt to farm beyond raising a patch of corn and pumpkins, a vegetable garden, and a few cows and hogs that provided for themselves by grazing and foraging in the woods for mast. These mountain people depended largely on wild game for meat, and they mastered the art of making whiskey as a primary means of survival. Whiskey served them in two ways: first, as a medium of exchange in a barter economy; second, as one of the few means by which the people earned cash.

The primarily noncash, self-sufficient economy of the entire study area lasted throughout the nineteenth century and well into the twentieth. To illustrate, Reuben Coffelt was "one of the biggest landowners in the Waterfall area" during the post–Civil War years. He purchased 300 acres at the foot of Roberts Mountain for "three quilts and a hogface rifle" but later told his granddaughter that he "worried from one year to the next how he would get the 60 cents necessary to pay his taxes." Subsistence farming remained the dominant economic pursuit through the 1930s, although many families across the area still engaged in hunting and gathering activities, and in grazing valley farmers' livestock on mountain grass and mast in exchange for an occasional free animal or a cash handout. The primary means of obtaining a little extra cash after 1900, however, were seasonal logging jobs, annual trips made each fall by some of the men to work in the midwestern corn harvests, and bartering or selling moonshine whiskey to friends and neighbors—who could ill afford the commodity. Like Reuben Coffelt before them, people during the first three decades of the twentieth century still worried about making enough money to pay their taxes and to provide an adequate supply of food and clothing for their families.

Because of the scattered nature of the population, people necessarily forged meaningful and enduring relationships with other members of their nuclear family and with their extended kinship group. The localities they occupied became intricate matrices of kin relationships, and created little worlds that reached out only a few miles in any direction.[8]

Such pioneer families were essentially independent, or at least interdependent within the extended family structure. Non-relatives in the vicinity were not as important in the scheme of things as family members; indeed, they were sometimes treated in an unfriendly manner, as indicated by the number of homicides that took place between neighbors and acquaintances across the years. Local people had contact with persons located elsewhere in the area only at irregular intervals, as when it was necessary to go to the nearest store, which might be located three to six miles away, for merchandise and supplies that could not be produced at home.

Very few persons in the State Line country during the last century traveled more than once a year to the distant villages that constituted their county seats. A few of them reputedly never made the trip from home to town, but these were exceptions rather than the rule. Everyone looked forward to the irregular visitations of traveling salesmen, politicians, and itinerant preachers, and to receiving occasional letters by mail. Some of the families were financially able to afford a few books, magazines, and newspapers. Others were not so fortunate. When I asked three people in a joint interview how many State Line killings were described in the local newspapers, the first narrator responded, "Well, I don't know, we didn't have no paper then"; the second person observed, "To tell the truth, I don't know whether any of it did or not"; and the third answered with both an illustration and an explanation:

In 1912, we lived over there on Bear River and my stepdaddy was a regular politician. He just wanted to know who was elected president or to any office right now. It was a long, long time before we ever heard of Taft being elected as President of the United States. He was elected in November, I believe it was, and it was way in the spring before we ever heard it.

A lot of the killings went unpublished. Didn't have no way of publishing it then. We all lived in communities before these roads were built. And something that happened in that community never did reach this community. The news stayed within the community unless somebody would be passing through and let us know.

The second narrator added, "If anything happened that you was a few miles from, maybe you'd never hear about it."

Because of the varied topography and isolated settlement patterns, then, the people of the State Line country did not necessarily share a common history of events and crises. Narrators' present lack of information about killings that took place in other localities within the study area attested to this fact. They had usually heard about fatal altercations elsewhere, but they were seldom able to provide in-depth, insiders' perspectives on them. Clearly, local talk about local violence was not intended for outside audiences. While a limited number of the killings enjoyed the status of subregional sagas and were voiced about in all of the State Line communities, most of the accounts remained at home, confined to the repertoires of local storytellers and their listeners. The presence of the multiple political boundaries figured prominently in narrative patterning and narrative distribution as well, as these lines, however arbitrarily drawn, were very important in helping people identify with a certain geographic locality. It was only natural that people in Trundle County, Tennessee, for example, spent considerably more time talking about crimes committed on Honey Creek than about violence that took place across the mountain in Hat Hollow in neighboring Brake County, Kentucky. It will be argued later that the presence of several political boundaries provided for the increased possibility of criminal acts. Certainly, local storytelling repertoires about violence attest to the fact that such boundaries played a significant role in the development of local culture.

The irregular nature of the terrain, coupled with the distance to their four respective county seats, caused the people to go without the benefits of law enforcement officials and attendant legal institutions throughout the nineteenth century. A subregional oral culture resulted, and endemic codes of behavior and social regulation developed in response to this lack of institutionalized law. Early churches in the area attempted to arbitrate disputes among their members, and even handed down monetary fines on occasion. The lack of formal law notwithstanding, there is every indication that local society in the pre–Civil War period was adequately stable and not given to lethal violence.[9] Oral tradition did not mention a single homicide during the first 50 or so years of settlement, and Rev. A.B. Alford, a circuit-riding Methodist minister from the Bear River Valley, corroborated the notion of a relative calm across the region in his published diary, which chronicled the period from 1844 to 1892. His first mention of violence and killing in the area occurred in August, 1858, when a church service was disturbed in the Bear River Valley by an altercation between three local Fountain County men and Flash Troxwell of Owenton County, Kentucky, who killed one of the three men with a knife, and severely wounded another. Alford noted that Troxwell was on trial for murder "when the war came upon the land."[10]

The Civil War brought infrequent passage of armies and small bands of soldiers through the area, but no major battles or skirmishes were fought locally. Nonetheless, the Bear River Valley was soaked in blood as a result of unrelenting guerrilla activity both during and after the war. Former United States Secretary of State Cordell Hull, a native of the general vicinity, described what took place during that trying period: "For several years during the Civil War, bands of guerrillas and bushwackers operated back and forth across the borderline, pillaging, robbing, and killing. They stripped the entire area bare of livestock and movable property. Only old persons incapable of military service, widows and small children were left at their homes. To them life was a perfect hell."[11]

Not even older men were safe from torture and death if they had sons who had enlisted in either the Confederate or Union Army or had joined an enemy guerrilla band. Oral tradition was lucid on this point, and Alford's diary corroborated the oral accounts of myriad killings committed throughout his Bear River homeland by the opposing cutthroat guerrilla bands of Confederate Flash Troxwell and Unionist Doug Beary, a native of western Fountain County. Alford identified by name, and often in great detail, 24 men (12 on each side) from

The old church and cemetery in Bear River Valley

the Bear River Valley alone who died at the hands of the guerrillas. Some of the victims were soldiers home on leave, including four brothers in the Union army; others were killed because of their sympathies for one side or the other. There were at least a dozen additional killings committed in the immediate area during the war. It was said that people often did not attend the funeral of a family member or close friend for fear the bushwackers would ride by and claim yet another victim. Leaders of the guerrilla bands maintained that their companies had been formed to protect themselves and their families from the enemy, but, in the words of a local historian writing in 1922, "These guerrillas developed into savage warriors and anarchy was the law of the land."

In the study area, as elsewhere across the Upper Rutherford region, the years following the war were filled with strong prejudices and bitter, divisive hatreds. Men who had fought on opposing sides of the conflict, even in the regular armies, were called upon to go home and live together in harmony. That was a difficult task, however, as the postwar state governments with unionist persuasions had neglected to adequately help these beleaguered counties when aid was most needed.[12] Local citizens, who had generally remained loyal to the Union, watched helplessly while their educational and judicial systems fell into disarray. Order was accomplished in due time, but the bitterness of those first few years after the war was intensified by the continued activity of certain men who had been members of the wartime guerrilla bands. These bellicose individuals continued to roam the woods and to lie in wait for their victims: those on the opposing side who had managed to survive the war years. The Bear River, Honey Creek, and Waterfall localities were hit hardest by the postwar violence. Matters got so bad in the Bear River country that Tennessee governor—and staunch Unionist—William Brownlow, commissioned Claborne Beary on April 1, 1868, "to raise, arm, and equip" a company of ten men and put an end to the violence and harassments[13] in the area, caused mainly by Sherwood "Sherrod" Bede, Jesse Bede, Carl Clifton, and perhaps a Merton—known collectively as the Bede gang (or Bear gang).

The Bede gang was apprehended but—given the unsettled political situation in Fountain County at that time—was apparently allowed to escape and regroup. One prominent resident decried the situation in a letter of July 8, 1868, to Governor Brownlow:

Owing to some dissentions [*sic*] in our party we had the misfortune to elect M.R. Marshall a prominent conservative sheriff at our last election. Recent developments tell me that he and others of his party are disposed to shield if not to aid and encourage the lawless among us. I refer particularily to Jesse Bede and his immediate associates. I am advised and believe he has permitted one of the Bede gang to escape from his custody and now permits the wounded Bede (his prisoner) to retain his arms. The Bede gang are to his knowledge and in his name gathering arms. Tuesday of our court he [Millsaps] publicly declared that he and party would band together and drive the Radical [Republican] party out of the country and said afterwards that if he was forced to leave the country he would know who to come back and kill.

About the same time I was requested to sign a petition asking you to disband Beary's company and reciting that the lawlessness of our county was merely a family affair between Bede and Parrigan when it was known to some who were circulating it that I with others had been threatened and that the gang was pressing and gathering arms.

Formal actions taken by Brownlow did not bring peace to the troubled area, as waves of killings committed by the Bede gang and others—sometimes referred to by local people as wars—kept the people of the area in a state of fear for several years after Appomattox. Any effort to reconstruct the events of those years chronologically would be virtually fruitless. Some of the narrators recalled hearing accounts from their parents and grandparents of the large number of killings that took place, but they were generally unable to say by whom or when. They did recall that some members of the Bede clan were involved in fatal episodes with members of the Holt, Washam, and Parrigan families, among others, resulting in several shooting and stabbing deaths on both sides. A fragmented reconstruction of some of those events follows.

Elijah Bede, the son of the area's first Bearcat Bede (a locally famous pioneer), lived on Bear River. It is said that two of his four sons were northern sympathizers and two of southern sentiment. Flash Troxwell's Confederate gang assassinated Ron Bede in late 1863. Doug Beary's union guerrillas ambushed and killed Jeff Bede in June 1864. It was believed that Preston Holt, one of Beary's guerrillas, bushwacked young Jeff in retaliation for the shooting death of Holt's father there in the valley during the war. Pres Holt himself was killed in 1866 or 1867 after he argued with Willie Crokes, the man who had married Jeff Bede's sister Nancy. It was assumed that Crokes was the one who killed Holt, as he immediately left the area for the seclusion of a Michigan logging camp. He was eventually found, arrested, and brought back to Jessetown to stand trial. The first night of Crokes's imprisonment, a band of men led by the Holts broke into the jail, bound Crokes, took him to the top of a mountain overlooking the Bear River Valley, tied him to a horse's tail, and filled him with bullets as the horse raced down the mountain dragging the body.[14] One narrator believed that at least a dozen additional deaths took place during the Bede-Holt trouble but could not produce the names of the victims. Another person corroborated the claim with the words, "I don't know how many they did kill." It appears that these comments regarding the Bede-Holt war are relevant only to the Civil War era and the immediate aftermath, as no additional oral recollections or printed sources mentioned any prolonged continuation of it.

By the mid-1870s the war-related violence had ceased, only to be replaced by general mayhem initiated and perhaps perpetuated in many instances by men who had learned the act of killing in guerrilla activities during and after the Civil War. Members of three or four families are mentioned in connection with the trouble that occurred during the late 1870s and 1880s, but four of the sons of Ron Bede of Honey Creek figure most prominently in present oral repertoires that tell of those times. They were Sherwood "Sherrod" Bede (b. 1844), Jesse "Jes" Bede (b. 1846), Bill Bede (b. 1851), and Poley "Pole" Bede (b. 1855). Sherrod and Jes had been Union guerrillas in Doug Beary's company of "independent scouts" during the war. Jes was involved in a gunfight with the father of Cordell Hull (the secretary of state mentioned previously) and shot his eye out. Sherrod was the prime mover in another shoot-out at a store in Brownsville; his younger brother Wash was killed accidentally as a bystander. In spite of or perhaps because of the incessant gun battles in which the four brothers were involved, their mother "Sukie" was always there to care for their wounds. Her nephew recalled that "she doctored her sons whenever they got a gunshot wound" and often boasted that she "could have saved President Garfield when he was shot" if she could have been at his side.

While the reputed Bede-Holt war during the postwar period has not been adequately documented, a Bede-Washam feud is a well-established fact. In describing the latter trouble, which is of unknown origin but may have stemmed from the hostility of the war years, a narrator who was born on Honey Creek in 1890 recalled the older folk saying that the Bedes and Washams were "into it all the time. When they'd come together, they'd have trouble. And Mart and Marion and Duck Washam, and Jes, Pole, and Sherrod Bede all got into a shooting match in 1888 in the garden where we later lived. And two of the Bedes hid from the Washams and laid there injured for two days before the Washams found them." Another narrator who was present during that interview claimed that "one of them went to a neighbor's house, and the woman was there alone. Bede was seeking shelter. They was after him. Said that there was a bloody handprint that stayed there on that neighbor's door." With that shoot-out, the Bede-Washam war apparently came to an end.

Pole Bede is the earliest person in the study area to be identified by the narrators for his involvement in moonshining activities and subsequent encounters with federal revenue agents. His whiskey still was located in the Clovis Christie Hollow just above Brownsville. When Carl Deadmond betrayed Bede by leading two lawmen to the site of his operation, Bede shot and killed one of the agents—a man named McDonald from Worley, Kentucky—and sought out and killed Deadmond not long afterward. Himself wounded with a gunshot in the arm, Pole "scouted around" (stayed in hiding) for approximately two years before finally being captured and imprisoned for two years. Due both to the Bede-Washam shoot-out and Pole's trouble with the law, he and other members of the nuclear and extended Bede family sought sanctuary in 1890 on Tennessee Ridge in Casey County, Kentucky, where the rugged terrain closely resembled that which they had left behind on Honey Creek. Pole died there at age 82 in 1937, and numerous descendants still live in that area.

Jes Bede was among those who moved to Casey County, but he was accused of returning almost immediately to Honey Creek and stealing 16 hogs from Ish Christie. Christie's son Braunley, along with a Washam fellow from Honey Creek, had moved to Casey County about the same time as the Bedes. While the three migrants were working at a sawmill there, an altercation between Christie and Bede resulted in Christie's death. The victim's half-sister explained what took place:

Jes Bedes had stole 16 head of hogs off my dad. And he drove them from Tennessee over to Kentucky and sold them. My dad took out a warrant for him. That was in the spring of 1890. I was born in December 1890.

The Bedes had left here and moved to Casey County, Kentucky. My brother Braunley and his wife had moved up there, too. And Jes and Braunley got into a fuss. Braunley called him "a damned hog thief," and Jes shot him.

My daddy never did get any money for the hogs, but there was never any more trouble after Braunley's death.

On an undetermined date, probably in the early 1880s, Baylor Christie (cousin of Ish) killed Lance Plinkett as the result of an earlier disagreement. The killing took place at Running Springs, located on the state line two miles west of and just across the mountain from the head of Honey Creek. Plinkett was married to Mary Holt, but her relationship to the Holts previously mentioned can only be assumed. She later married Cleo Billings who was also bushwacked at the head of Honey Creek. The same narrator who provided an account of the death of her brother shared what she'd been told about the axe slaying of Plinkett:

I got this through my mother. That's been a long time ago. And I've heard her tell it, and I've heard my grandmother tell it. It was Lance Plinkett and High Christie that had trouble. And High Christie and his son Baylor Christie hauled goods for the stores around through that part of the country [Honey Creek]. And they had been hauling from Washington.

And Lance Plinkett was a-moving his family, I think, to Missouri. And he waited. He sent his wife Mary and his sons on ahead in the wagon with her brother to Worley. Landon Holt was the woman's brother. And Lance Plinkett, the way mother told it, and two of his friends, Carl Emory and Carl Waltham, stayed back and waited till just about the time he would meet these Christies at the state line.

So they met up there. And they got into an argument again, and Plinkett was planning on shooting the old man Christie—High. And his son Baylor picked up the axe and cut his, well, cut his head about half off they said. They borrowed a handkerchief from my aunt and it was tied around Plinkett's throat after he was struck with the axe, mother told me.

So that's the way that went. . . . Now that happened over there above what they call Running Springs, up that road toward where Dr. Carnes's home is now.

The father of this narrator, Ish Christie, was himself guilty of murdering a man back in 1869. A person with roots in the Mt. Gilead area, near where the killing occurred, recently provided a Brake County newspaper with two oral traditional versions of the killing of Peter Tripps by Ish Christie. Both were printed in the same newspaper account. The Tripps version is as follows:

One night about 1869 Peter Tripps, son of Eli and Elizabeth Young Tripps, was ambushed as he rode his horse into the yard of the family home on Bingham's Fork of the Little Piney Fork area of Brake County. Tradition has it that he was shot off of his horse by a man named Christie, who was hiding in a large tree, patiently awaiting Peter's return home.

In order to avoid further bloodshed, Eli decided to migrate to Jasper County, Iowa, where some of his wife's brothers and sisters had previously settled. Eli and family left Worley, Kentucky, in April, 1870 and arrived in the Rock Creek Township of Jasper County, Iowa 36 days later. This story was told to me in July, 1971, by Thomas Jefferson Tripps, a grandson of Eli Tripps.

He stated that notwithstanding the efforts of his grandfather to avoid more bloodshed, that his father and Eli's son, William Franklin Tripps, heard of his brother's death. He returned to Kentucky on horseback to find the killer of his brother and revenge the death. After days of hard riding, he arrived on Little Piney Fork to learn that Christie was no longer in the country.

A Christie version of the shooting varies somewhat:

At a party or gathering of some sort on Little Piney Fork, Pete Phillips [actually Tripps] hired an old woman to poison the whiskey. Several young men were made sick from drinking this whiskey and Sammy, son of Isham Thomas Christie, died. His father later killed Phillips and had a price on his head in Brake County. He hid out in Fountain County, Tenn. for a while, but one day he saw the old woman, who had poisoned the whiskey. This caused him to flee to Canada where he stayed a year before returning to the Little Piney Fork country. Apparently, he was never arrested or tried for this act, although several men were seeking the reward for his arrest.

Again, it was Ish Christie's daughter who, disagreeing with portions of the newspaper account, related the family version of the incident on at least four different occasions. She was especially incensed at the notion that her father was hiding in a tree, awaiting the return of Tripps. The following composite text is based on her exact words:

Sammy [Christie] and Pete Tripps was both dating the same girl. They had been to a dance on the Piney Fork close to Mt. Gilead. And my brother had drank some whiskey, and they found him laying at the spring, dead. And they thought that the girl and Tripps had went in together to give Sammy this poison whiskey to get rid of him. The girl that was supposed to poison the whiskey was the sister to the one that Sammy and Tripps was a-dating. They was Burkses. Her name was Emaline Burks.

So my dad went to this young man's house, and he had gone to the corn mill. And my dad tied his horse to a tree in the yard and set down on the porch with his pistol across his lap, waiting for the boy to come back. When he rode in, Dad shot him and killed him. He fell off of his horse in the yard.

After Dad killed Tripps, they put out a $50 reward. Back then that was a fortune. And, of course, he was expecting somebody to come and arrest him. So he left and went to Canada and bought a place. He fixed up a house and cleaned out a well, and came back here and was planning on taking his family.

Well, he stayed around on Rutherford Mountain and scouted around for a while, I reckon, to get his business fixed up to get ready to go. And he stayed in a cave. His wife and children fed him. And he said they was a path running along pretty close to the cave. And said he was setting out in the sunshine one day. Said he heard somebody coming tipping along. And he said he looked up there and said it was Emaline Burks. Said she was right at him before he seen her. Said he thought she'd turn him in, you know, tell Tripps's dad.

So he left out of there and he come down on Honey Creek and bought a farm on Honey Creek. Just left that farm he bought in Canada, never did go back up there. Moved his family down there on Honey Creek; it was in a different county. They was a reward put out for Dad. And there's where they come to try to arrest him. Three men came over from Kentucky to arrest him.

Well, he was upstairs unloading wheat. Back at that time they put their wheat, when they threshed it, upstairs. He was up there unloading the wheat when these men come to arrest him. He always kept his gun with him at that time. So he come down—they was a-coming in to go up to him, and he come down with a gun. And they tried to shove the door open with the barrel of a gun. And his son-in-law was holding the door for these men to get away. So they went out and the son-in-law told them, says, "You'd better get away." Says, "He's dangerous."

So they went out and two of them got on their horses. And the third one told that son-in-law to hold the door and he'd go too. So he was in such a hurry he didn't put the bridle up on the horse's neck; got it up on the side. And they didn't come back to try it no more.

Christie himself was shot and killed in 1902, but his death had nothing to do with the foregoing chain of events. That is another story and will be told at the appropriate place.

Sometime after the Civil War, Bartin Billings (generally called "Bart") reputedly killed a woman and threw her body in a hole on the mountain above his house. The woman had spent the night in Billings's home in Buffalo Lick Hollow, located in Trundle County. Ish Christie's daughter also knew of this killing:

[Bartin Billings] was a pretty rough customer, according to what I heard his wife tell my mother one time. She said at one time they was a woman that come to their house to stay all night. She was going through to Washington and was walking. Bart said, "I know a nearer way that we can go through here. I can take you out up toward the top of the mountain and cut off a lot of ground."

Said next morning her and Bart started out. His wife told my mother that that woman never was seen or heard tell of any more. They was a big hole up on the head of Buffalo Hollow. She said that that woman was killed and put in that hole. . . . Said she had money.

And Garland [Boyer] and Gary Boyer used to keep hogs back on the mountain. The mountain was covered in mast, all kinds of acorns and everything. Well, they'd buy up a bunch of hogs in the fall of the year and take them back there on the mountain and turn them loose, you know. And they would camp around out there and take care of them and see after them.

And these Talbots—Annis Talbot and Cleve Talbot—watched after these hogs when they wasn't around. Garland said they was camping one night not too far from where this hole was and he said there was some of the most pitiful groaning and hollering and taking on that he ever heard in his life at that hole. He said that they never did camp there any more. That was years and years after the woman had disappeared.

Another narrator provided additional details about the woman's death:

Now when my granny was just a little girl, she went up there to spend the night. Well, they was some woman come along there and she had $800 in gold, to stay all night. She was going down through Waterfall.

Well, she wanted to get started the next day before daylight; she had a long ride, you know. Well, Bartin got up, you know, and went on his way in front of her. I reckon there's a cave up there. He killed her and cut the horse's throat. She had an old mammy dog, you know, and the mammy dog had pups.

I've heard my granny tell about it, said, "She's there." Come back the next morning, but she stayed all night there at Bartin's. And he's a-washing the blood off his hands. Said, "Ain't many men can make $800 before breakfast!"

A third person present when the story was told agreed with the basics of the account and strengthened the supernatural element: "He killed the woman and threw her in the Booger Hole."[15]

A brutal double murder occurred October 26, 1886, in an isolated cabin on Bat Cliff Mountain in Brake County between Mt. Gilead and the state line. The victims were Jarvis Tunk and his sister Mary Ellen, ages 42 and 38. Although neither was married, they, with Ellen's eight-year-old son, lived together as a family.

Their killer was Bronston Nesbitt, a shiftless resident of the interior of Rutherford Mountain, who lived on both sides of the state line, depending on where his mother Suzanne was able to find shelter for herself and her three sons, Bronston, Doug, and Bull. Bron, as he was called, sometimes worked as a farm laborer but most often did nothing more than roam the countryside. On occasion, he may have helped the Tunks with their livestock grazing practices.

I interviewed approximately a dozen narrators regarding the motive for the crime, the actual killings, and Nesbitt's subsequent public hanging in Washington, Kentucky, in January 1887. Most of them said that Nesbitt, upon learning that the Tunks had sold some steers, went to their place for the purpose of robbing them. Others said that Nesbitt was working for the Tunks at the time and that Nesbitt enticed Jarvis Tunk to go with him to the spring, where he had hidden a jug of whiskey. Nesbitt stabbed Tunk to death; then, finding no money, he went in quest of Ellen to force the money out of her. Upon her inability or refusal to produce it, Nesbitt tried to choke her. Because of her size, Ellen successfully resisted his efforts until he delivered a fatal blow to her head with a washboard.

Thanks to the attacks by the Tunk family dog, Ellen's son was able to get away from the assailant, who had sought to murder him as well. The boy made his way to a neighbor's house and told the gory tale, and it was his testimony at the trial that convicted Nesbitt.

On the gallows, Nesbitt reportedly lectured the crowd on the perils of whiskey, offering the sorry end to which he had come as testimony to its evils. He never broke down emotionally, however. Dressed in a suit with collar and tie, he walked to the gallows without assistance, remarking, "I can make it; I'm not dead yet." It is said that Nesbitt refused to have a hood placed over his head on the grounds that he wanted everyone to see "the best-looking man that was ever hanged," but he disallowed his wife's request that his children be permitted to witness his death—to which she retorted, "You never did want your children to see anything."[16]

The presence of whiskey and the ease with which it could be procured was a constant precipitating factor in the area's homicides during the last years of the nineteenth century and in later years as well. To observe that everyone in the State Line country had ready access to illegal whiskey would be to understate the situation, as virtually every nineteenth-century family made or used whiskey on all social occasions, for medicinal purposes, and as a medium of exchange in economic dealings. There were few, albeit some, cultural admonitions and voices raised against its use. The creation of the temperance society in the Bear River Valley in 1845 attests to the fact that some local people were concerned about whiskey consumption, but there is no record of any violent deaths caused by alcohol prior to the 1858 event in which Troxwell stabbed and killed a man on Bear River.

Indications are strong that the local whiskey situation was kept in check until 1873, when Congress enacted legislation requiring that licenses be purchased and taxes paid on distilled whiskey by all who made it. That act was nothing new; it was simply a reaffirmation of one passed during the presidency of George Washington to force the American people to help pay the costs of the Revolutionary War. But although big distilleries had been compelled to pay the taxes, the law was not enforced against smalltime operations. Many stills on the frontier, including those in the State Line country, had gone unlisted and thus untaxed until enforcement of the new law began.

Aside from economic and practical considerations for opposing the tax measure, local people resented the federal government's restriction of a practice that had been handed down for generations within the family. Why, they asked, could they not dispose of their corn in any way they saw fit? Why should making whiskey at home be viewed as a criminal act? Nonetheless, home brewers who did not pay their taxes were transformed overnight into outlaws in the eyes of federal agents.[17]

When the Internal Revenue Department set about in 1873 to enforce the new law, people in the Upper South had their first introduction to revenuers. Federal agents did not flock into the State Line country in quest of offenders, as they had to deal with the reality that any person in the area who made whiskey on a commercial scale would shoot first and ask questions later. Yet some inroads were made by the agents, with the result that moonshiners removed their stills from streams near their houses and hid them in secluded hollows, thickets, coves, and caves. (Producing whiskey in this fashion was safest at night, and easiest on moonlight nights; hence the name "moonshining" throughout the region.)

The revenue act of 1873, coupled with the lingering effects of the Civil War, must bear its share of the blame for the violent character that came to be a hallmark of State Line culture. If culture is "a set of traditional value orientations conducive to certain patterns in situational behavior,"[18] the post–Civil war period in the State Line country was ripe for the development of a culture in which homicidal behavior would be accepted as a way of life. The absence of law and order during and after the Civil War created a situation in which social control, as exercised by area residents, was devoted to self-protection.[19] This situation was aggravated when the federal government passed alcohol control measures that prompted an acceleration of hostility toward civil authority. A people torn asunder by guerrilla warfare and placed constantly on the defensive against threats to their very existence were not ready to surrender to federal agents whose presence threatened their economic and social structure. When the moonshine stills were secluded from the eyes of the law, changes occurred in drinking habits. People, who once consumed their own whiskey in controlled amounts, turned to periodic heavy consumption of the substance which they were now compelled to purchase, yet could not really afford. Economic and social tensions resulted at home and abroad, with the men relieving their anxieties and emotions by drinking heavily, talking loudly, behaving boisterously, and fighting freely. Sometimes they killed in the process. These characteristics of violent behavior continued to plague residents of the State Line country for the next 70 years, and have even stamped indelible marks on the culture of the 1980s.

2

The Self-Sufficient Years

THE YEAR 1890 represents the approximate date to which current oral traditions reach back in time, thus marking the beginning of the area's recent history from the insider's perspective. The narrators had a "feeling" for the years that have come and gone since that time; they or their parents frequently knew firsthand about living conditions and various killings, which they described with unflagging interest. The coming of the entrepreneurial sawmills about 1915 symbolized the beginning of the end of an old way of life in the State Line country, for logging and sawmilling marked the introduction of cash employment for many men of the area and signaled the demise of a self-sufficient, family-based economy.[1]

Early in the period the residents were still closely in touch with the customs, institutions, and ways of living that had marked the settlers' culture from the beginning. There was nothing in 1890 to indicate to them that things would ever change, and there is no indication now that they had the least desire to be a part of the social change that lay just over the horizon. To these people, their culture was stable. They lived in harmony with nature and with the land that sustained them. The family was still the unit around which basic social activities revolved; social class divisions were minimal; socializing beyond the walls of the home still took place within the immediate locality; the economic structure was still largely

An Owenton County family near Tall Rock at the turn of the century

based on a combination of hunting, farming, and moonshining; moonshine whiskey was still consumed as a matter of routine; healing of the sick was still a domestic responsibility, although trained physicians were becoming more readily available; schools and churches were weak but growing; there was still a marked absence of structured communities; and killing was still done quickly and quietly in defense of property, family, and personal honor.

The family was most important in shaping the attitudes and actions of area residents and in serving as the focal point for social interaction. The extended kinship network was important in the overall social and economic framework of each locality, but the concerns of the clan (a term never used by the local people) were never as significant as those of the nuclear family. For example, the fatal altercations to be described later

never motivated reprisals by anyone other than members of
the immediate family, and even they were not always involved,
as most of the killings were interpersonal (one on one) in
nature. Death generally ended the matter, especially if the
local code saw the killing as justifiable. Such was the case as
recently as 1970, according to one narrator:

> A dispute over a boundary happened a few years back in Fountain
> County. A boy had bought up a lot of that land out there and he got
> over on the other fellow's property. These were young men, too. This
> one that killed the other one was over about ten feet on him; had set a
> rock. And they got into it over ten feet of that old mountain land and it
> ain't worth a dime an acre. And this one killed the other. Said, "I'll go
> to the house and get my gun and I'll come back and kill you." And did!
> It wasn't very far from where he lived.
> So he went back and killed the boy there. There never was nothing
> said or done about that. They compromised. No arrests were made.

The nature of sex roles and domestic relationships within
the home were important above all other considerations. Parents spent countless daylight hours with their children at work
in the home and in the fields and woods, often no more than an
arm's length away from each other. During cold winter days
and long nights, family members moved about and slept in
extremely confined spaces. There was no such thing as privacy
at any time of the year, not even for courting couples. On the
surface these mountain people perfected the art of living in
harmony with parents, siblings, and often a grandparent. It
may be that the lack of privacy was a precipitating factor in the
violence experienced here across the years, but that position
will not be argued in this study. For now, it seems sufficient to
describe the living conditions that were common throughout
the State Line country, and to do so from the memories of
persons who had lived through those times and recalled them
with considerable nostalgia. The following descriptions are
varied in content, but taken as a whole they provide a glimpse
of life prior to 1915.

One articulate narrator was born at the turn of the century
and lived his first nine years in the mountainous terrain at the

head of Bingham Branch. In telling about his family's encounter with a threatening rattlesnake, he provided a graphic look
at the way they lived at that time:

We was tending corn back in an old mountain field back there at
home. And my daddy had Suzanne Nesbitt staying there watching the
bees. He had bees and bee gums. And he had her there watching them
so that when they swarmed she could holler us in from the field, and
he could put the bees in a gum.

So we heard her screaming and hollering and taking on. (My
parents always took my brother and me to the field because we was
awful aggravating. You know how kids are.) So we run to the house.

And, you know, people fattened their hogs in pens then. They
always floored the pens to keep the hogs from eating dirt, you know.

Well, when we got there, we was looking for the bees a-swarming in
the bushes or around. She met us at the gate and said, "Mr. Beardly!
Mr. Beardly! They was two big old snakes right there! Right there, a-
fighting!" Said, "One run under the house and one run under the hog
pen."

Well, we tore the hog pen up and killed the one that was there. I
think it was a copperhead. And the next day, we come in from the field.
And my mother always lay down in the bed to take a nap before we
went back to work. And my dad went way off over there to a big spring
to get a jug of water to take back to the field with us.

And us boys was aggravating Suzanne while Mam was laying there
asleep, or trying to sleep. And it was an old puncheon floor. There
wudn't hardly no lumber back then to floor the houses with, and them
puncheons was wore slick. (You know, they used to scrub the floors
with sand and a scrub broom. I've made many a scrub broom.)
Anyway, Suzanne would get us by the coattail and give us a jerk, and
we'd scoot way back to the bed. That would just do us a bushel of good.

Suzanne could smell a snake. And she would go to the fireplace to
get a coal to light her pipe with. And she'd peep and look for a snake.
She'd say, "Sho-o-o, I smell a snake."

So Mam couldn't sleep, so she decided to get up and look all around
there. And if they wasn't no snake there, to make Suzanne set down.
So she got up and looked in the big meal barrel behind the stove. And
she looked in behind that big meal barrel and there lay a big old snake
coiled up, half way up that barrel.

We had an old .56 Civil War gun, and if we got into trouble and
wanted the others to come quickly, we always got out and shot that old

gun. Just had a few shells. And Mam run out in the yard and shot that old .56, and dad come a-running with the jug of water, just nearly out of breath.

So when he come in the house, he run over there and looked behind that meal barrel, and there lay a big old snake coiled up halfway up the barrel. He got the gun and shot its head smooth off. (We'd covered up the barrel so nothing could get in it.) And he shot its head plumb off. Then he pulled the barrel out, and here come the snake a-wallowing out on the floor with its head plumb off. We didn't know where it was for a long time. It was a big rattlesnake. And I forget how many rattles and buttons it had, but it had a big bunch of them. So we got to hunting for its head, and its head lay in the door to the kitchen with its mouth open. And, boy, it had a great big mouth! And it could have closed it up on a fellow and it would have been a sight.

But instead of Mam being mad at Suzanne any more, she was proud.

That narrator had married a woman from the Hat Hollow section of Brake County, and together they shared personal recollections about family sex roles during their own childhoods:

Wife: I was Archie Coffelt's girl. I grew up right down the hill here. I had two brothers and two sisters, and father was a farmer. He also run a sawmill and a gristmill. When he went to the field, the women went right along with him to help work. Chopped out corn, hoed it.

Montell: Did your father help around the house?

Wife: My mother mostly done the housework. He got wood and things like that.

Husband: My family all worked together. See, back then we foddered beans. We'd grow big patches of beans and we'd string them on a string and dry them. . . . We'd all work together. My father, too.

The daily work routine for two families on Honey Creek is described in the following accounts:

The women went to the fields. Made a garden and went to the fields to work. Yeah! My mother helped tend the crops the same as my dad. They took the children to the field with them. Had a pallet in the shade to take care of the kids. They had snake dogs to watch out for the children.

Mother cooked while Daddy fed the stock. And sometimes she got our dinner the same time she got our breakfast. Just warm it up and eat it. We'd eat breakfast about daylight after we'd milked the cows and fed the stock. Then we went to the field and worked till about 11:30; come in and eat. Then, we'd go back and work till about 6 o'clock or sundown.

I worked in the field just like my husband did from the time the corn was planted. But, now, I never did plow corn. That's one thing I never would take hold of. But from the time that corn was planted till it was put in the barn, I worked just like he did.

My mother lived with us the rest of her life, and she raised my kids. She never went to the fields. She took care of the kids, raised the garden, and did the washing. She had a lot harder job than I had. She would pick blackberries and things like that, but she never filled a can. I done all the canning.

And back then, if the kids didn't make their toys, they usually didn't have any. The boys made sleds and wagons to play with. They would go to the woods and cut sled runners or cut a small sapling for wheels if they wanted wheels instead of runners. They would saw four wheels with a stand saw and make a wagon large enough for a 12- to 15-year-old boy to ride on. Little children played with wagons made with wire and spools from sewing thread. Boys usually got knives by age ten, and the girls played with homemade dolls. But, now, some of the girls got dolls from the stores if they had money to pay with.

Although the workday was from sunup to sundown, and all family members were expected to contribute labor at their particular levels of expertise and ability, oral evidence indicated that some men who manifested laziness might be disciplined by verbally aggressive tactics, which, if not heeded, were followed by more violent practices such as flogging and switch-whipping. In response to my question as to what families did when the head of the house did not work to support them, a narrator stated emphatically, "They would steal." Theft, too, was thus present but not usually so readily admitted to by the narrators. To have acknowledged thievery would have had the effect of openly criticizing a neighbor or close acquaintance, and this was seldom done. One person claimed that people never stole from each other, but recalled in the same breath that families had padlocked their cribs and smokehouses for as long as he could remember. However, "Uncle Ben Emory was different," he recalled. "He didn't lock his store on Honey Creek. Said he didn't want the store tore down. Said, 'They could get what they wanted and get out.' " Narrators' claims to the contrary, it was some form of theft that precipitated a substantial number of the homicides described throughout this study.

Given the inadequate space in most houses and the size of the families occupying them, sleeping arrangements always necessitated two or more beds in the same room. One narrator recalled that her childhood home had three beds in the "main room": her parents slept in one, her grandmother in another, and she in a trundle bed. Another narrator stated that she and her sister slept in the same room with their parents until the sisters were married. A male informant observed that he slept with his mother until he was 13 years old; his brother, four years older, slept with their father. I asked him if he ever felt the need for privacy during those years. "Well, not too much," he responded. "You see, if you ever take off from home, you'll crave it. It's just what you grow up with. The life you grow up with becomes a habit." Perhaps his last statement goes far in explaining the unconscious acceptance of violence in the culture.

I asked him and his wife how parents at that time managed to be alone together. With a nervous laugh, the woman responded, "I guess when the children went to school." Her husband then commented, "They took special care of their girls. In old times, you couldn't sit in the parlor with a girl unless there was someone who could see what was going on. We grew up under an atmosphere like that. Fathers took special care of their girls. They didn't go out like they do now. If they went to church with a boyfriend, there was someone of the family that went right along to watch and guard." Another narrator who grew to manhood in Hat Hollow claimed that fathers there "would blow your head clean off your shoulders for fooling with their girls."

Courting couples near Tall Rock, 1928. The women were sisters.

Despite this protective attitude, illegitimacy was common in the study area. Unwed mothers raised their children at home under the considerable shame of social rather than individual condemnation. In one instance, a child listed on the 1910 census for Honey Creek as a boarder was actually the illegitimate granddaughter of the householder. The girl's mother also lived in the household, and she was correctly identified as the daughter. A child of unwed parents carried the name of the mother, who typically received no child support in any form: "Most of the men [fathers] just turned the woman and child loose." Child-producing adultery, too, was documented in numerous instances, but society condemned the practice then, and people today are usually silent on the subject. Often, it appears, neither the offspring nor the wronged spouse ever learned of the transgression. One man from Brake

County, however, reportedly took his new baby home to his wife to be raised along with their other children.

Punishing children was typically the job of the father, although there were instances when the men abrogated their responsibilities. Resulting tensions were no more intense under these circumstances, however, than when drunk fathers struck their children for generally unjustified reasons. The general care of small children was the responsibility of mothers until an older daughter could take charge of them.

Orphans were parceled out among families in the area, generally their own kin. Since adoption papers were unheard of, names were never changed. Orphan boys were kept by the foster family until they were 21, at which time they were "turned loose, if they wanted to go, with a good horse, a bridle, and a saddle. That was the rule. The girls got household items when they got married."

Since very little "new blood" came into the State Line country across the years, kin relationships became quite complicated. There were numerous examples of weddings involving first cousins, even double first cousins; two or three siblings from one family marrying siblings in another family; a survivor marrying the spouse's brother or sister or mother or father; and numerous members of one extended family marrying members of another family over a period of 35 to 50 years. Between about 1880 and 1920, for example, 25 Washams married Emorys in the Honey Creek area alone. An extreme instance of complicated familial relationships involved two brothers who married two sisters, became parents, swapped spouses, again had offspring, and then returned to their original spouses for the remainder of their lives.

The absence of viable communities in the study area in early years, coupled with relative isolation from the county seats and mainstream society, resulted in the creation and development of strong-willed individuals and families but, at the same time, permitted the growth of a society that fostered egalitarian attitudes, beliefs, and practices. Although some of the families had more possessions than others, social class lines were not drawn except in three or four instances to be noted later. When queried regarding the social standing of one of the seemingly beggarly troublemaking families in the vicinity of Honey Creek, the narrator responded, "They was like the rest of us up there. They lived about like we did." Another informant, who was born at the head of Bingham Branch, recalled, "We were just in the general run of people. There wasn't no rich people, hardly. And there wasn't no poor people. Awful scanty. People lived pretty good back then, I'll tell you they did! They didn't have money, but they lived in a different attitude." Such democratic tendencies and sentiments of the nineteenth century conflicted with twentieth-century social realities brought about by the commercial lumbering, sawmilling, and oil drilling operations that came onto the scene just before and shortly after World War I, providing considerable opportunity for employment and increased social interaction.

Despite the rough, low mountain terrain, which dictated a scattered settlement pattern, the people of the State Line country from 1890 to 1915 were, in general, able to help each other during periods of social, economic, and emotional need. They swapped farm labor, held house and barn raisings after disaster struck neighbor or kin, and cared for each other in times of sickness and death. One person remembered those days of sharing with these words:

Neighbors helped each other back when I was raised up. When anybody got sick, the neighbors went in if it was crop time and finished up the crop.

They set up with the sick at night. The families would take turns. When they died, the women made the women's clothes. And they bought a little thin suit for the men; buried them that way. Didn't break up nobody. They did all that themselves. They always made their own coffins. That's the way they put them away.

If anybody had a burn-out, the neighbors went in and built the house back.

People used every available excuse to interact socially with the families around them—that is, if they wanted to be friends with them. They went to church together, or they worshiped in groups on large, flat, bare rocks and along stream banks when churches were too far away. They walked or rode together to and from church, and they engaged in fellowship around "dinners-on-the-ground" following preaching services. People went to church in those days as much for the socializing as for the spiritual experience. So it was, too, with the activities centered on the local school. Pie suppers were especially popular as a form of social interaction, as they provided needed opportunities for festive behavior and budding courtships, in addition to raising money to buy chalk, erasers, ball bats, maps, and other items for the school program. These occasions were not always without boisterous actions, temper flare-ups, and weapon brandishings, however, when too much whiskey was consumed or a rival purchased a certain girl's pie box.

Children often gathered at one home on Saturday or Sunday afternoons to play various forms of ball and games like Skip to My Lou, Sugar or Tea, Drop the Handkerchief. Even sweethearts with serious thoughts about their future together often participated in these events, which gave them an excuse to spend some additional time together away from the watchful eyes of parents. One narrator provided this account of the gatherings at her home on Honey Creek:

When I was young—well, grown, we'd go to Sunday School, then go back home in the evening [afternoon]. Every kid in the country would gather at our house on Sunday; they'd go to the neighbors' house the next. I have known of as many as 64 children there at one time.

We had a big apple orchard just as shady and pretty. We'd get out there and play all evening. The kids would just gather up there. Sometimes some of them would go home with us for dinner.

The mother of this bunch across the creek, she'd get out and play with us. That's what me and Garland [husband] would do when we first started courting. We'd play out there with the rest of them.

Young adults often went in small groups on foot, horseback, or in a jolt wagon to a picnic site near a mill dam or some natural landmark, such as a cave, bluff, or rocky crag overlooking the countryside for miles around. Some courting occurred at these outings, but the events were mainly designed to give

As the photograph at right (c. 1895)
illustrates, guns and banjos were
almost always in evidence at social
gatherings in the State Line country.

Below, this group of young people on an outing from Honey Creek
(c. 1921) included Christies, Lyonses, Talbots, and Washams.
Talbot (center male, back row) is the only one of them to die in a
shoot-out.

the participants an extended visit with their peers without interference from younger siblings and parents. Younger and older adults alike, if willing to face condemnation for their actions by the more sanctimonious populace, also went to dances at which fiddles and banjos supplied the music, whiskey was consumed in abundance, rowdy behavior was commonplace, and killings occasionally occurred. These effervescent events were racially integrated by the Curtises and Prathers, the only known black families in the study area following the Civil War. The following description provides insight into the nature of the social interaction at these dance events:

> Well, Old Miss Yancy danced, and she was up in her 90s then. She'd dance all night if anybody would dance with her. Her and this man danced every tune that they played that night.
>
> And they had their liquor set up on the counter, and you went and drunk any kind you wanted—different kinds, you know. And none of them got too drunk; just had a big time. Everything went off peaceful that night. But Pitt got killed sometime after that. On this particular night, they's just having a good time. They eat Burl Coffelt out of house and home that night. And dance, it was a sight!
>
> These Prather Negroes down below Mattis lived over there by the old Riley place. There was Kirk and Gary and Coats, and the old woman [mother]. And people would go there and take them some liquor and stay three or four days. They danced away their farm. Had a pretty good farm there. And that old woman would take a few drinks and dance up a storm. They all danced.

Visiting the scene of a crime was an additional, if bizarre, social pastime for both men and women. A woman from Honey Creek recalled that if "people heard that someone had been killed, they'd flock to the place like a bunch of buzzards. And women would go, too! I went to one or two murders myself." Other narrators commented, perhaps to justify such visits, that many people went not only to witness the proceedings but to offer help to the bereaved when needed.

The concept of community in the study area was slow in developing, and the actual communities there at the time were vaguely defined by the dispersed residents in accordance with a family's proximity to a school, a church, or especially a store, since many people attended neither church nor school on a regular basis. (What schools and churches there were at the time were poorly developed and struggling, as people rarely thought of giving money in support of either.) Using the presence of a store as the essential criterion for the existence of a community, Brownsville, Mattis, Bell Fort, Waterfall, and Stonybrook can be so identified as of 1890 and since that time. Collectively, these communities form the western perimeter of the State Line country. The hinterland contained no communities, as commonly defined, because of both the rugged nature of the terrain and the practice of looking upon the nuclear and extended family as the most meaningful social and economic units. Rutherford Mountain did have several geographical entities, however, which will be referred to as "localities" for convenience only, and defined as those areas identified by the families who occupied a more or less continuous area of land and who had fairly frequent social interaction with each other. It was such localities as Tall Rock, Honey Creek, Buffalo Lick Hollow, Hat Hollow, Rocky Valley, and Grandview Rockhouse—as well as Waterfall—that produced the bulk of killings across the years.

The churches in or adjacent to the State Line country that served as gathering points for people in the area were located at Mt. Gilead (pre-1810), Waterfall (1840), and Rocky Valley (1896) in Kentucky; at Sinking Springs (1823), Pleasant Hill (pre-1830), and Brownsville (1888) in Tennessee. It cannot be argued that area killings had their roots in a time period when there were no churches. They were there all along, at least to a limited extent, and itinerant ministers also traveled through the countryside at irregular intervals, conducting marriages and delayed funeral services. Nineteenth-century churches sometimes held courtlike hearings to arbitrate disputes among their members, and attempted to regulate behavior in general; overall, however, they were unsuccessful as agents of social change. Although they attracted people from miles around to their religious services, and although hellfire-and-damnation sermons frequently brought sinners to their knees, the churches were incapable of changing the violent atttudes and actions set in motion by the Civil War and subsequent events. Actually, they were hard put simply to survive as places of worship. Rev. A.B. Alford, describing a "basket-meeting" he attended with a group of believers at Waterfall in the 1870s, concluded, "The church at this place has been for a long time in a low state of religious life."

The rowdy element in the area frequently disturbed religious services by hanging around outside, drinking, shooting guns, cursing, and conversing in such loud voices that the preacher's sermon could barely be heard above their continuous din. In 1905 the Brake County *Reporter* published a Warrant of Arrest authorizing any sheriff, constable, coroner, marshall, or policeman in Kentucky to take into custody J.A. Black for interrupting the worship service at Waterfall in "the manner of the idolators of old." The charges against him included "loud and lordly, boisterous and boastly, unwise and otherwise sorts of language and languages, both living and dead; he did accuse and demean, and abuse divers members of said congregation charging said persons and members with divers and various crimes and misdemeanors such as adultery, thievery, stealing of stove caps from women's cook-stoves, fornications, stealing hog heads and hog faces, laundered shirts, etc." Obviously, the accused—tanked up with whiskey—had gone to the church and called out the names of most persons present inside, accusing them of hypocritical behavior and singling out their rumored sins one by one.

Such unruly constituents dominated most social events in the State Line country by the 1880s and retained charge of affairs through the 1930s. They accomplished this by raising profane voices unleashed by moonshine whiskey, traveling in crony groups, riding roughshod over the countryside on horses and mules, and flashing knives and guns at the drop of a hat. A man who reputedly ranked among the roughest ever produced in the State Line country told me that "most everybody was

Baptizing at Lightsboro, Kentucky, c. 1910.

rough back there in them days. Most of them carried guns."
Another narrator, who also knew what he was talking about,
testified, "People back there drunk a lot. Had nothing to do but
just lay around and play cards and get into trouble. Shoot one
another."

Two statements relevant to Trundle County, gleaned from a
local newspaper in 1896 and 1897 respectively, reveal much
about the unlawful demeanor of the times. The first observed,
as if in surprise, that the "Circuit Court passed off quietly"; the
second stated that "during a gathering of the roughs at the
house of Logan Steen near Shelltown, Sherman Mallory was
fatally shot. The little brown jug was conspicuous at this rally."
In 1904 the Brake County newspaper reported informatively
that "quite an amount of mean whiskey was in evidence this
Christmas and several individuals were on the war-path, but
no one was seriously injured and the day passed off more

quietly than usual." The June 1904 session of the Brake County Circuit Court issued 70 indictments, 50 of which were for making or selling illegal whiskey. Available court records around the turn of the century contained a few indictments against State Line men for carrying concealed deadly weapons, disorderly conduct, and similar other charges. Yet none of the accused were involved in actual litigation; they had either fled the area or their accusers—perhaps fearful of retaliatory action—were unwilling to testify in court against them.

Viewed as a whole, the State Line country produced an impressive list of killings during the years 1890-1919. Given the lack of court records and of persons with knowledge of all the crimes, obtaining an actual count was virtually impossible. I documented some 20 violent deaths and feel strongly that a realistic figure is 30 or more. Likewise, all efforts to identify the killings that occurred within a given locality were unsuccessful because the narrators were unsure of the exact location of some of the altercations. In other words, an episode that occurred "back there on Rutherford Mountain" could have been at the head of Buffalo Lick Hollow or just a half-mile away at the head of the Emory Branch of Honey Creek. Bear in mind that most of the narrators were too young at the time to know and recall the exact site, and those who did know would not always share precise details with me for one reason or another.

The Honey Creek vicinity, wih its numerous families, produced the bulk of the killings just before and after the turn of the century. This is not surprising, given the fact that the Ben Emory store on upper Honey Creek and the Triton Milner store in Brownsville acted as magnets, pulling people in from Mattis, Bedes Branch, Buffalo Lick Hollow, and other nearby localities. The personal character of these visitors was seemingly no different from that of the people who lived on Honey Creek; they were all mountain people, to use their own term, and generally of the same socioeconomic status. But they gave such a rough reputation to Honey Creek that it continued to be thought of in these terms until the 1950s. One person commented, "They's been a lot of killings and bushwackings on

Honey Creek, but it ain't as bad as it used to be." Another, whose parents grew up and married on Honey Creek, felt that it was "worse than Hackney [two miles away]. It used to be a sort of moonshine country. Three or four made whiskey up and down Honey Creek, and a lot of people drank." A native of Bedes Branch recalled what it was once like to travel down Honey Creek: "Used to, if I went from home to Mattis, I'd have to fight my way there and back. Now, though, kids can go down Honey Creek and not get into it with anybody." Finally, a person from the opposite end of the county shared his recollections of Honey Creek in the 1920s, when he worked in the area as a surveyor: "All of them hollows and creeks up through there were full of old jugs and kegs and things like that. There was a whiskey bunch that lived in there, you know, for years."

Alcohol, like theft in its various forms, accounted for many of the area's killings. Whiskey was not always a precipitating factor, however. Sometimes it was a boundary dispute, as in the instance of a son shooting his father over on Rutherford Mountain about 1900, for which no legal action was taken. A close relative recalled the event:

My sister, Mary Jane, married Jes Gant. Now that Gant killing, I know why it was done. It was done over a boundary line between land. Bill Gant killed his dad when they got into a fuss over who owned so much land. It was over a line on Hardman Mountain.

That was on the same mountain that Dad [Ish Christie] was killed on. I've passed the place many a time. I was always scared to death because they said it was haunted. My sister [Mrs. Mart Bede] lived on up past that place. And when we'd go up to her house, we always had to pass right by where the killing took place.

They was a pond up there they called the Gant Pond. I guess it's still there. It was on through the mountain. You didn't pass any houses until you got way up on top.

Now, I don't think anything was ever done about that killing.

Another narrator recalled the event, but mainly in connection with the ghostly gunshots heard at the scene:

Well, I can't quite put it together, but a boy had killed his daddy there. And my mother and Leona Pannings and another or two went there to stay all night. And they said at exactly midnight they could hear an old muzzle-loading gun, you know, go to pounding, pounding the bullets in. And said that gun would go off. You've never heard such a gun in all your life! And she said she absolutely heard it, and I know she did, for she didn't lie.

One of the most talked-about killings in the Honey Creek area occurred on May 28, 1902, when Frank Bowles shot and killed Isham Christie in the Bowles Hollow, located just east of Brownsville, to avoid the consequences of hog theft. (It was Christie who had killed the Tripps fellow back in 1869.) Bowles was dating one of Christie's daughters against her father's will. The "rough name" of the Bowles family, who were ne'er-do-well tenant farmers, may have been at the heart of her family's opposition. Tensions heightened after Christie found one of his two-year-old steers dead in the pasture and ordered Bowles not to carry a gun while crossing his land. Christie's daughter provided the following description:

About a week after the dead steer was found, several hogs belonging to the daughter of Carl Boyer turned up missing. She had a bunch of shoats that she'd put back in that hollow. Back then, they would get fat on mast. And the hogs was all gone, and somebody told her that the Bowleses had killed them and salted them in a cave. The Bowleses lived in Bowles Hollow way back across that mountain from Honey Creek. I never would go over there after Dad died. They were stealing hogs. That was the trouble. . . .

Well, Uncle Carl Boyer went to Magistrate Tom Washam and took out a search warrant to go over there and search and try to find this meat. Well, he deputized my two brothers, Jes and Carl Christie. And Carl Boyer, Tom Washam, Jes and Carl and Dad all went over there. Dad told them, "I don't want to make this trip. I don't feel like that walk." It was a long walk over there; about three or four miles. They all told him if he didn't go, they wudn't going. He said, "Well, if that's the way you feel, I'll go." So he went.

And they went on up on this mountain. And my sister and her husband, Mart Bede, lived up there within a mile of where this killing took place. Well, they went on past Mart's and they deputized him. So they all went on over there. Well, the dogs run on ahead and went to Bowles' home. And when they got down pretty close to the house,

Frank was a-setting by the side of the road—a little path—with a shotgun across his lap, barefooted. Said when they got up pretty close to him, him and Dad got into an argument. I don't know who passed the first word. Dad called him a "damned sheep-eyed devil." And when he done that Frank shot him. And then Frank started to run, and he was going over, they said, a steep hill. And my brothers shot two or three shots at him, but everybody said they shot over his head.

Christie's five companions left the scene; his two sons went for the sheriff, and the dogs kept everyone away from Christie's body until Isham Faris, a relative who had been working for Christie, got there and calmed them. The body was hauled away in Christie's own wagon, and he was buried in the Brownsville Cemetery, in what his daughter remembered as the first factory-made casket she had ever seen. Bowles, concealed in the loft area of one of Christie's own barns, watched the solemn proceedings.

When the sheriff found Bowles—after four or five days of searching—the accused was taken to Shelltown to appear before Magistrate Dale Rigney, who reputedly released him in exchange for $10 and a gallon of whiskey. Upon learning of the payoff, Christie's youngest son went before the grand jury and asked for an indictment against Bowles. That body upheld the request, and Bowles fled to Alabama, where he was sheltered by his parents, who had recently taken up residence there. Sheriff George Crutchfield and his sons went to Alabama in a horse-drawn carriage, apprehended Bowles, and brought him back to stand trial. He was sentenced to a ten-year term in the state penitentiary.

In March 1984, Christie's daughter showed me a letter written to her in 1975 by the daughter of Mart Bede. It illustrated the indelible impact those killings had on the minds of family members and friends, and admirably showed that these matters are still very much a part of the psyche of the people there. In part, the letter read: "I heard the gunshot that killed your father. My dad was present, as you know. Nothing has ever slipped my mind that happened. And I passed the place where your father killed Tripps every day as I went to school at Grandpa Sharpe's."

Sometime about 1907, Roy Slayton shot and killed Cleo Billings. Both were residents of Honey Creek, probably in the Bedes Branch section. Billings was the son of Bartin Billings, already identified as the killer of the itinerant woman whose body was tossed into a hole. Cleo was listed on the census of 1900 as having been born in 1859; his wife, Mary, was born in 1852. They had two sons at home, born in 1884 and 1888, respectively.

Roy Slayton was born in 1873 into a family of low character and reputation that was involved in several killings on Honey Creek. Roy married Eula Bede, daughter of Pole Bede, and they had two sons. Some narrators believed that Eula was seeing Cleo Billings on the sly; others avowed that she was not, that Roy only thought she was. At any rate, he chose to eliminate his presumed rival by shooting him from ambush and making Eula witness the death of her lover. The killing occurred as Billings and his wife were coming up Honey Creek in a jolt wagon, sitting side by side in the seat.

When that happened, me and my sister was going up on the mountain to another sister's home. And we was way up through the field when we heard the shot that killed him. It was about a half-mile above where we were. And we also heard the wagon and team running away after Roy shot him. But we still didn't know what it meant, not till we got the news about it.

That was the wagon Billings was in. He was driving the wagon. Him and his wife was setting in the front seat. And they's some other folks setting behind them. They'd been to Hackney to some kind of celebration or something.

And Roy was standing beside the road in behind a little sycamore tree—well, you might say a bush. He stepped out, they said, and spoke a few words to Cleo. Cleo stopped the wagon. And as he started, Roy drawed aim at the cross of his suspenders and shot him.

And my brother-in-law had been up on the mountain before that. He was hunting some sheep that he had lost. And Roy and his wife— Roy's wife was cussing this brother-in-law of mine, Mart Bede. And he said they'd come up together on the mountain, and he said that Roy had his gun that he'd bought to shoot him with, Mart said. Roy was jealous of Mart, too, like he was of Cleo. I think that was the main reason. And he said that Roy kept his gun trained toward Mart, and said Eula would shake her head [no].

Slayton was arrested, convicted of the killing, and sent to the state penitentiary in Nashville. Eula left the area soon thereafter and never returned. While in prison, Roy began working as foreman in a cookstove factory, and upon release he stayed on with the company until he was ready for retirement. Eventually, he returned to his old home on Honey Creek to live out his days. A former sheriff and neighbor recalled raiding Slayton in the 1950s to confiscate his moonshine still and to arrest him on a whiskey-making charge. In an authentic display of warmth, the sheriff explained that since he was "fond of the old man," he sat down and talked with Slayton while the deputies demolished the still. Slayton returned the show of friendship by giving the sheriff a treasured square blue bottle he had obtained while in prison.

Cleo Billings was buried with Masonic rites in the Brownsville Cemetery. Not long afterward, it is said, his ghost returned to the Billings home each night, stood at the front gate, and hollered out to family members. The Billings family persuaded Carl Black, a neighbor, to come to their house and talk with the revenant in an effort to get it to leave them alone. He tried but was rendered powerless to speak at all in its presence. Black even cut a hole in the front door through which to communicate with the ghost, but he was still dumb as long as the supernatural being was there. It was not long before Mary and her two sons grew weary of the unwelcome visitations and moved to Missouri to live among relatives.

The next celebrated killing on Honey Creek took place on May 3, 1913, when another of the Bowles boys earned his niche in oral tradition by brutally murdering a landowning, recently widowed, 65-year-old black female resident of the area. The killer was Homer Bowles, Frank's younger brother; the victim was Cindy Curtis; the place was Ben Emory's store. The event was recalled by Emory's nephew, who visited the scene of the crime:

I went to see her when she had been killed up here at my uncle's store. She'd been at the house washing for my aunt, and she came over to the store to get her pay. My aunt was sitting on the inside of the door, and this old Negro woman set down on the outside of the door on the porch.

This Bowles boy was there, and there was another woman [Bess Talbot] and her daughter [Lura Lee Talbot] there, and he'd been dating this girl. All of them was barefooted, you know, and Bowles kept pointing his gun at the girl's feet. This old colored woman was there, and he turned the gun on her and let it go off. On purpose.

This fellow Homer Bowles that shot her was setting down on the edge of the porch with his gun laid across his arm. His gun went off and just blowed her whole head off. Shot her eyeball out. It was sticking on the side of the door. I seen that sticking on the wall. It blowed her brains all in my aunt's hair and everything. And there was a dog that come around, packing a bone. . . . And it was blowed out of her, just as dry as your hand. Brains and all blowed out.

Although Bowles maintained that the shooting was an acci-. dent, he was convicted and sentenced to serve time in the state penitentiary at Nashville. None of the narrators questioned his guilt, but virtually all of them believed that Bowles had been hired by Cindy's nephew, who had been living with her and stood to inherit the property at her death.

The Slayton, Billings, and Bowles families were all from Honey Creek or nearby Rutherford Mountain. Additional families in the same locality produced a certain breed of young men who collectively raised hell and effectively ruled the area with fists, knives, and guns through the 1930s—the Nesbitt, Talbot, Lyons, Well, Sands, Baylanch, Husted, and Pannings families, among others. "The people in that area carried guns," commented one narrator. "It was just handed down to their children. Their fathers carried them. Grandfathers." Another volunteered, "They was rough, and they'd do just about anything. Wasn't too much done about it by the law either." Between the ages of 17 and 25, these young men—clad in overalls, denim trousers, or "Sunday pants"—roamed the countryside in groups of four or five, as a narrator from the area recalled:

Just a gang would gang up that way. When I was a young kid, boys was awful bad to gamble. You take the Talbot boys, Ben and Len and

Lug, and them Lyons boys and Husted boys, and all of them joined in together, one of them making whiskey and the others doing this and that. They was a gang.

Fifty-eight years ago [1919] when I was riding horseback coming over here to see Nina, I run into a gang of them. And I didn't know what I might encounter before I got through them. But they was always good to me; never did try to hurt me in no way."

The gangs sometimes rode horses and mules, or simply traveled on foot. One of the Talbots of Rutherford Mountain boasted of their prowess as teenagers at walking and running across the mountain terrain:

When we went anyplace, we walked! We didn't mind walking. We was so stout and so tough, if we had a mind to we'd just light out and go plumb to White Oak [12 to 15 miles away]. We'd just light out and walk over there. When we got ready to come back home, we'd just walk. A horse couldn't outrun us in them days. I could outrun a horse. I've actually run against horses!

Sometimes, we'd get into a wrestle—play and wrestle some—us and a bunch of them boys from Rocky Valley who'd come out there [to Grandview Rock House] to be with us. We'd get out there on them big high ridges and, boy, you talk about running! Un-uh-uh-uh! Shit, I've run them ridges just like a big fox time after time. Jump the cliffs. I jumped over a cliff one time and jumped right on top of a big rattlesnake. Here the others come after me. Some of them was like hounds, you know. They'd run you, you know. Yeah, they was bawling like hounds after me. But they couldn't nothing-like catch me!

I killed the rattlesnake. Yessir! Killed him with a big club—a big stick, I think it was.

Killing was generally a private matter with the Rutherford Mountain contingent, but there were exceptions: on two or three occasions some of them teamed up to ambush the enemy. Also, there was a Nesbitt and Talbot vendetta that almost reached feuding proportions. The quarrel between these two hunting-grazing-moonshining families originated around 1900. They lived close to each other on Rutherford Mountain on opposite sides of the state line, equidistant from Tall Rock, Hemp Hollow, Buffalo Lick Hollow, and the Ben Emory store.

The Nesbitt line known in oral traditional memory begins with Suzanne Nesbitt, who was probably a Pannings before marriage. Suzanne's husband was unknown to oral sources, and her own name was not included on the federal census rolls. She was remembered as a "low, heavy-set woman, who wore glasses and kept her head tied up with a handkerchief all the time like old people went," and lived to be over 100 years old. She spent her entire life on Rutherford Mountain, drifting from house to house in her later years in quest of food and shelter. The last cabin she occupied was located at the head of Skillet Creek and is reputedly haunted by her ghost.

Suzanne's three children all lived recklessly and died violently. Bronston "Bron" has been described already as the person who died on the gallows in Washington for killing Jarvis and Mary Ellen Tunk. A second son, Bull, gave his own son a new gun with which to kill a Talbot; he was later gunned down himself. The third son was Doug, a legendary hunchback who was robbed and killed by decapitation at the hands of a great-nephew in the 1940s. A younger narrator from Honey Creek recalled having heard that "the Nesbitt family was low-class people; one of them was so low that any house he was about to move into was burned the night before." Another person said, "They were pretty rough people. The Talbots were about the same way. It was mostly the old set of Nesbitts that was bad, and it run down through the young generations. But it was the younger Talbots that was bad. They'd crossed blood with the Nesbitts."

The Talbots had occupied Rutherford Mountain for 60 years or more prior to the outbreak of their trouble with the Nesbitts. Traditional family genealogy starts with Benuel Talbot and Susan Black, residents of the Bear River Valley, whose marriage produced three daughters (Sally, Alta, and Trish) and seven sons (Parton, Carl "Bull," Thurgood, Acie, Annis, Cleve, and Carley). Descriptions of their physical appearance hinted at a reputed if unverifiable Indian ancestry: "Their hair was shoulder length and just as black as a crow"; they had "red faces and hawk noses"; "they looked Indianlike with greasy hair and greasy faces"; "the girls have got just enough Indian blood in them to make them look pretty."

Alta never married but had five children and raised them on Rutherford Mountain at or near Grandview Rock House. Most of the others also produced children, generally born in the 1890s, who harassed the countryside for the next 30 to 40 years and were regularly involved in killings, both as perpetrators and victims.

The first trouble of record between these two families occurred in early spring of 1903 when Elbert "Eb" Nesbitt bushwacked Thurgood Talbot. Nesbitt's age was unknown, but Talbot was about twenty-seven at the time. Thurgood was married to Eb's sister Sally, who was one year younger than he. They had been married for nine or ten years, as a son had been born to them in 1894. Thurgood and Sally lived in a board-and-batten shack at the head of Buffalo Lick Hollow not more than a mile from her parents. There is every indication of prior trouble between Thurgood and his father-in-law, Bull Nesbitt, as oral testimony claimed that Nesbitt promised his son Eb a new Winchester .32-.20 rifle if he would use it on Thurgood. "They was something back in those days! That was the highest-powered gun that had ever been in this country."

Eb Nesbitt went to Buffalo Lick Hollow and, standing on a cliff while aiming through a fork in a dogwood tree, shot across a hollow into a small clearing where Thurgood was outside his cabin, either making a wooden toy for one of his children or holding a baby. One narrator claimed, and another corroborated the account, that Talbot was "setting by the side of the door with a baby [Shirley] in his arms. They didn't have any porch, and he just put a chair on the outside and was setting down there by the side of the door with the baby in his arms. Somebody shot him, they said, from the hill up above the house and they laid it on Nesbitt."

"How in the world he ever killed him that far with that rifle, I don't know," said another narrator. "We've looked at that place a lot of times hunting or cutting timber. He shot him standing on this cliff way across this hollow. And he was hunkered down. They was a cleared place [field] there where they could make a little stuff to eat. . . . He shot him and killed him all that distance from over there."

"The Talbots wasn't bad people," the first narrator volunteered, "but they was mixed up; got mixed up by marrying into families that was pretty rough. Now, Thurgood Talbot's wife was a Nesbitt. Maybe that's why the trouble came up. . . . It was talked just as rumor through the country that Jes Bowles did the shooting. It wasn't long after Talbot was killed that Jes Bowles married his widow."

People in the Honey Creek–Brownsville area always suspected that Bowles was the illegitimate son of Acie Talbot. If Bowles was involved in the shooting, then, he helped to kill Thurgood in order to marry his uncle's widow, Sally, also a close relative. Jes's brother Frank was the one who had murdered Isham Christie the previous year, and it was Jes's son who later killed Doug Nesbitt, the hunchback. "Sal" subsequently had an illegitimate child by Carlson Brannan, whose own son Joshua killed a man during a lover's quarrel in a sawmilling camp in Buffalo Lick Hollow in 1925.

There is indication that Trundle County officials got wind of Thurgood's death and offered a $25 reward for the capture of Eb Nesbitt. He fled immediately into the deep recesses of the Hat Hollow section of Brake County, where he hid out "in a little hut down in the woods." A few weeks later, Thurgood's brother Acie, with revenge burning in his chest, began a tenacious quest of Nesbitt. With him was Otis Beary, grandson of Doug Beary, the Unionist guerrilla chief during the Civil War. Some narrators, including Acie Talbot's nephew, said that Otis Beary was there as a deputy sheriff from Trundle County; others, including two of his first cousins, claimed that Otis went along only to collect the reward money. One narrator, who was born in Hat Hollow about the time the killing took place, visited the scene of the crime in later years. Here is the way in which the account of Eb Nesbitt's death had been described to him:

[It was] a few Sundays later [after Eb Nesbitt killed Thurgood Talbot] up there in the forks of Bran Hollow and Hemp Creek—right at the forks. I've seen the poplar stump. It may still be there. One Sunday morning, Eb Nesbitt come down through there walking. Old Acie Talbot, I guess he was the oldest brother of Annis and Cleve, him and this Beary from down on Honey Creek was down there. And they told Nesbitt to halt, and he made a dive to get to this big tree. But he killed him. They said Beary is the man who killed Nesbitt, but he ran off and left.

Well, they never did hear from Beary any more. Talbot went on back to Tennessee where he lived. Might not have lived too far from his brother Thurgood that Nesbitt killed.

They [Kentucky officials] arrested him [Talbot], and he come back across the line, didn't put up no resistance. And the governor of Tennessee found it out. He said, "They'd have never took him as long as I lived, and I'd of left it where they never could of took him back. I'd have given him a permit to kill ever Nesbitt that crosses the state line into Tennessee."

Acie Talbot's nephew also stated that it was Beary who did the shooting: "My uncle wanted to take revenge against Eb, but the high sheriff from Shelltown said, 'That's what I get paid to do!' Then he shot Eb. . . . But Uncle Acie wouldn't rat on the high sheriff and had to serve some time in prison for it."

Talbot was 44 when he went to the penitentiary. After serving his sentence there, he moved to Washington, Kentucky, and lived with a woman in the Poortown section—known for its prostitution activities—and had a daughter by her. He eventually moved to Indiana, where he died at age 61.

Beary was never heard from again. A bench warrant for his arrest was issued by the Brake County Circuit Court on June 10, 1903; the warrant was returned unserved in July and October of that year, and again in October 1904. The hunt apparently ceased at that point.

Bull Nesbitt fled to California following the revenge killing of his son Eb at the hands of Talbot and Beary. No one knew the nature of his employment in California, but he returned to Kentucky about three years later "a rich man" and bought a farm in Hat Hollow that was commonly referred to as "the California place." "Granddaddy Nesbitt had a lot of land," recalled his grandson who, incidentally, is Thurgood Talbot's nephew. "He brought people in," he continued, "bossed them around and beat them with poles to get them to do what he wanted them to do."

Shortly before 1910, perhaps about the same time that Cleo Billings was killed on Honey Creek, Bull Nesbitt was shot and injured, for reasons that were not made clear, while walking up Hat Hollow toward his house. A man who grew up near the site picked up the story at that point:

Bull Nesbitt was coming up Hat Hollow. He owned much land there then. Had a big, long, white mustache. Carl Black fired on Bull and cut his lip and mustache off with the shot. Bull knew it was time to leave Hat Hollow. He went to Tennessee to live. . . . Went to a little town near Jessetown. And he told a merchant there, "Let the people have a little credit."

And he was pretty bullheaded, you know. He'd always tried to bully people around and he wouldn't pay that merchant. And the story went that they got on the outside—arguing outside the little store. And he started to pull his hand out of his pocket, and this merchant killed him. I don't know how many times he shot him. And when his hand come out he had a $10 bill in it. He was going to pay the merchant all the time—just wanted to bluff a little.

Another narrator explained that Suzanne Nesbitt, Bull's mother, received news of her son's death by direct revelation from God:

Suzanne was staying at our house. And she went up in the hollow above our house one evening and we heard her praying and shouting up there. And she come back to the house and told us that somebody had killed Bull. "Bull Nesbitt is dead," she says. "Bull's dead." She kinda played like she was one of these psychics. And now she was pretty good at it because God revealed that to her.

So the next day we heard that a man out there had killed Nesbitt.

Located just north of Brownsville and west of a line drawn between Buffalo Lick and Hat Hollow is Tall Rock, even more celebrated in oral legendry than either Honey Creek or Rutherford Mountan. Tall Rock itself stands in Kentucky, roughly on the line between the two Kentucky counties, and the state

Early morning mist from Honey Creek almost hides Brownsville in this photograph, taken from Tall Rock.

boundary runs at its base. This precipitous cliff, dominating the surrounding countryside and peering over the upper reaches of Honey Creek, is visible to Tennesseans for miles. It is not discernible, however, when approached from the north via the state highway, which winds through the rugged hill country of southern Brake County before dropping abruptly at Tall Rock down the south side of the mountain to the head of Honey Creek in Trundle County.

Tall Rock and the adjacent mountainous terrain were historically a paradise for moonshiners, and others who sought refuge from the law, from the 1880s to the 1950s and beyond. The area surrounding the rock "has always had a bad name," being known for its "stills, fighting, and all that stuff." Everyone was in accord about the large amount of whiskey traffic that took place there but disagreed about the number of bushwackings and killings that had occurred along the state line; estimates ranged upward from seven to two dozen (I have accounted for at least a dozen). One narrator exclaimed, "There's been a sight on earth of killings that's been around there." Another commented, "Up here around Tall Rock, they never died a natural death, not even yet." The seeming discrepancy in the total number of homicides there can be accounted for on the basis of geography. Some of the narrators were thinking only of a single whiskey-selling establishment when they heard the term "Tall Rock"; others thought of a somewhat larger area extending east and west along the state line to include the Rutherford Mountain localities previously identified.

However many killings there were, such incidents gave the residents around Tall Rock a reputation far and wide for being "different." In the words of a narrator who lives in Fountain County, several miles away, "There was some difference in the people who lived around Tall Rock and others in the county. Some Tall Rock families dealt in whiskey. They were pretty tough people. Had to be, they followed different ways of living." Area residents concurred. Tall Rock's reputation intimidated and frightened grown men. The following account imparts something of what one man once felt when he found himself alone at Tall Rock:

We all had hounds, and fox hunting is the greatest sport in the world. Well, we'd go to the Waltham fields at Tall Rock to hunt. And I was a sleepyhead. I'd lay down and go to sleep within 30 minutes after the hounds got to running.

Once when I woke up, there was old man Surly Deadmond's hat hanging on a limb right down below me, and his coat. And there had been seven men found dead and killed up there at the state line. Well, I woke up and there wasn't nobody else there. It was just as dark as pitch. Well, I wasn't afraid of nothing, but right then I was scared to death! And I got up and hollered a few times. Not a sound—man, dogs, or nothing. I was one-half mile away from any house. And the first thing was a bunch of woods to go through, and me without a light of any kind.

Well, I finally found a little path and I just drug my feet along it to see if I was still on the path. There I was two miles from home and had to travel over the roughest road that ever was through the woods and across gullies. And, brother, I give them down-the-road the next morning for leaving me.

Many families are identified with Tall Rock, but one stands out above all others as perhaps being responsible for the greatest number of killings in the area. That name is Hardcastle, a family whose log dwelling was situated astraddle the state line. The Hardcastles were descended from prominent Trundle County pioneers, but they dictated the character of the area from about 1900 to the beginning of the Prohibition era in 1920 by peddling whiskey and violence. Their name still conjures up considerable awe and lingering fear in the minds of State Line residents. A former county judge stated flatly, "The Hardcastles of Tall Rock were rough people," and a former sheriff used the word "bad" several times while talking about them. Two women remembered the Hardcastles as "a rough bunch of people," and a third recalled being intimidated as a child by the very mention of the Hardcastle name: "My daddy was a doctor," she said, "and he'd save all his empty bottles for them. And they'd stop and get a whole load of bottles at one time." She then continued in a lower voice: "I was afraid of them. One brother killed another brother up there when I was little. I was afraid to see them pass by in a wagon, afraid they'd kill me, too."

The particular family associated with violence consisted of Eagle Hardcastle, his wife Bertha, their children, and some in-laws. According to the federal census for 1900, Eagle and Bertha were both 43 years old in that year. Artema, their first and only daughter, was 19 at the time. Their first two sons, Tault and Balm, ages 16 and 14, had been born in Texas. William H., age 11, Crane, 10, Cleve E., 6, Claxton, 2, and Woosley (who was born after 1900) were all natives of Owenton County, Kentucky. Eagle died soon thereafter, leaving Bertha to care for their youngest children. The true extent to which Bertha contributed to the violent behavior of her sons is unknown, but most people believed that the Hardcastles did not engage in the whiskey business until after Eagle's death. Two persons were very strong in their indictment of Bertha for founding and perpetuating the illicit traffic, claiming that she even offered a round of drink to the men present at the burial of her son Crane, who died at the hands of his brother Tault. "My uncle said that Mrs. Hardcastle brought out a quart of whiskey and passed it around," one narrator testified, "but he said he turned it down. Said that's the only drink he ever turned down in his life." Unverified rumor about Bertha at the time influenced later oral tradition to the extent that one narrator, whose own father was making moonshine in the Tall Rock area during those years, claimed, "She would take a drink out of every jug of whiskey she sold. Sometimes she would drop little white pills in the whiskey while pretending to wipe off the mouth of the jar with her hand, and the men would die along the path. Poisoned! She killed seven people that way." Another informant strengthened this unverifiable rumor and the mystique that surrounded the Hardcastle family by claiming that "12 people were killed back there within a year's time about 1917. They would get them drunk, rob them, and then kill them." Perhaps the violence that Bertha allegedly spawned on Tall Rock was more than even she could handle. One narrator remembered the gun that she purchased for use in case a fracas got out of hand: "The Hardcastles' mother got her groceries at Stonybrook. And she'd stop at home and rest on the way back. She walked and carried a load of groceries. And she was talking about how some of them was carrying on back there. She reached in her apron pocket and pulled out one of them little old double-barrel derringer pistols called the American Bulldog. She said, 'I'm going to let my bulldog work some of these days.'"

Much of the Hardcastle land, still referred to by area residents as the Waltham place in honor of its prior owners, was located in Trundle County, but the house itself was partly in Kentucky and partly in Tennessee. "They lived there and bootlegged out of the house," recalled one narrator, adding, "They sold whiskey to Tennesseans in Kentucky and to Kentuckians in Tennessee." The physical relationship of the house to the

state line accounts for the following anecdote, which illustrates the dilemma in which law enforcement officials often
found themselves:

> One time the law come down there to the Hardcastles. The Hard-
> castles didn't have jugs to put the whiskey in. Had it in water buckets.
> The old woman grabbed two buckets and run out the other door into
> Tennessee. Just stood there and held it in her hands.
>   The Kentucky lawman said, "I'll be back for you."
>   She said, "I'll have another run made before you do."

Selling whiskey locally was prohibited by state law, yet the
Hardcastle whiskey operation at Tall Rock was legal under
Federal statute, as they had a government permit to make
whiskey and to operate a gauging house where corn liquor was
bought, taxed, and sold under periodic inspection by revenue
officials. In November 1914, Hardcastle whiskey unfor-
tunately got into the hands of young Claxton Hardcastle, then
only 15 years old, who became inebriated and killed his friend
Lyn Faris, who was staying at the Hardcastle home as a hired
hand. The first of two narrators who were present at the inquest provided the following account of the killing:

> Lyn Faris was married to a girl from Hat Hollow, old Preacher Carl
> Black's daughter. And this Faris drank all the time, and gambled. He
> hung out [stayed away from home] a lot of the time, played cards, you
> know, and drank. Him and Claxton Hardcastle had come down there
> on Honey Creek, down by Ben Emory's store, and they were drunk.
>   And they came back up the mountain and they got into a drunken
> brawl, and Claxton shot him.

The second narrator gave more details:

> Claxton and Lyn Faris got into it at Uncle Ben Emory's and Uncle
> Ben put them out of the store. Claxton was riding Garland Emory's
> horse. Claxton said, "I've got to take that horse on up there."
>   Uncle Ben said, "Hell, no! Take that horse on up home and bring it
> back in the morning."
>   They went out to get on the horses and got into it out there, and I

think Claxton slapped him with a pistol and the pistol went off. Aut Husted said that the two of them got on their horses and left.

The next morning, Woosley, Claxton's brother, brought the horse back home. Uncle Ben asked him, "What became of Faris?"

Woosley said he didn't know. Said, "His old mule was standing up there at the barn this morning." Said, "I don't know where he is."

Uncle Ben told him, "You'd better look for him." Said, "He's drunk."

Some other fellows went up the path—a nearer way to get up there [to Tall Rock]. They went up through there and they found a hat. They took it on up to Hardcastles. It was Faris's hat. Well, the next morning when they found Faris, they held an inquest.

Carlson Brannan lived up the road there. Him and his boy Joshua lived up there together. Well, Carlson come down there. They had a fire built up. I was there. Then after awhile Joshua come down over the hill. They was a snow on the ground. He didn't have no shoes on; had his feet wrapped in rags. He come running down over the hill [narrator chuckles], and Lyn was a-laying behind a log—beside of a log. Well, Joshua jumped up on that log and said [in a raised voice], "Where's he at?" And he looked down and seen him and said, "Hell, right here he is!" He took right back up the hill just as hard as he could go [narrator chuckles again].

Claxton spent some time in prison for killing Faris, then apparently lived in Chicago for a while following his release. When he eventually returned to Trundle County, he was a different person, it was said, with the resolve to live a peaceful life. Well-liked in his early years, Claxton was equally liked and respected in later years. He served as deputy sheriff of Fountain County in the 1950s and was remembered until his death in the late 1970s as a person with only the killing of Lyn Faris to mar an otherwise fine record.[2]

Despite what happened to Claxton, the Hardcastle whiskey industry flourished, as there was no other licensed operation closer than Barksville, located on the state line some 12 miles to the west.[3] The cloak of leadership among the Hardcastle brothers was jointly assumed by Tault and Crane to whom the six-year difference in their ages seemed not to matter. Their whiskey-making operation continued to grow until they had four stills going at one time, and a natural rivalry developed between the two brothers over production and sales. One narrator claimed that "Crane was selling whiskey up there above Tault, and Tault was a-selling down there. And there was just jealousy, and a dispute came up over it and Crane shot Tault. They got into a row and he shot Tault. That was about 1915."

Rather than accuse Crane for the attempt on Tault's life, another narrator stated simply, "Some of them shot Tault the day before. He was packing rocks to make a bond house to put their liquor in before it was stamped. Somebody shot him out of the woods—shot and hit this rock. Sort of wounded Tault a little." Whether the bullet richocheted and hit Tault or was fired directly at him, it went through the corner of his mouth and came out at the ear lobe. The wound "wasn't real bad" but did necessitate the services of "little" Dr. Prather, a young physician who lived three miles away in Kentucky, between Stonybrook and Lightsboro. Prather's decision to go to Tault's aid placed his own life in jeopardy. In the words of the first narrator:

He went up there to see Tault and they were in there when Crane came up to the door. And Tault Hardcastle grabbed Dr. Prather, just shoved him between himself and Crane. And he worked his way over to the shotgun that was sitting behind the door. And when he got around to it, he gave the doctor a shove out of the way and grabbed the shotgun and killed Crane. You know, those doors had great big cracks when they opened. He shot Crane through the crack in the door.

At this point in the description, the narrator's sister interrupted him to clarify the sequence of events:

He came there to kill Tault, and Tault was holding the little doctor in front of him to keep him from killing him. And Crane cussed and said, "I'll kill you." He told the doctor, "I'll kill you," and then let Crane have it. Shot his eye out. Killed him on the spot. And Crane fell right out the door and fell right under Dr. Prather's horse's feet. And it scared the little doctor so much that he got up and run off and left his horse hitched there. And somebody else had to go and get it.

Before he darted from the room, Dr. Prather told Tault, "I'm leaving here! And I ain't got no gun neither." Tault just went to his dead brother and took the gun out of his hand and gave it to him. Doc said, "You can shoot, kill, or do anything you want to, but you needn't to ever call me no more." Dr. Prather's flight was remembered by a narrator who claimed that he "passed by here on foot and, boy, was he flying!"

In flush times the Hardcastle whiskey stills were inadequate to produce enough liquor to meet local demand. Nor could such moonshiners as the Tarter, Westmorlans, and Roberts families be relied on extensively, as their operations were not licensed, and they ran the constant risk of being raided by revenue agents. On occasion, when the Hardcastles' whiskey supply ran low and their own stills were closed down, they placed an order with a licensed distillery located out of the region for a load of whiskey to be shipped by rail to a point on the Southern Railroad several miles east of Jessetown. The whiskey was then brought to Tall Rock in secrecy over treacherous mountain roads and trails to avoid detection by local authorities. One informant recalled a particular time when Tault was returning with a load of contraband whiskey:

Tault come on here one night. He was hauling liquor from out here—government liquor. He'd go to the railroad and get it. And just before his wife got killed, he come on here and his mules was give out. And he wanted Dad to take a pair of mules and pull him up the mountain. Dad told him, "I can't go."

I was a little fellow. He asked me if I could. I says, "No, I can't go."

Dad said, "I'll let you have the mules, a pair of mules to pull you up. Or you can get Carl Janis up here at the old store house to drive them on up there." He hollers up there to Carl. Carl says, "Yeah, I'll do it." He come on down and they geared the mules up, and Carl asks me, says, "You go with them."

I says, "I don't want to, much."

Carl says, "Well, go." Says, "We can get all the liquor we can drink." I said, "All right, I'll go."

We went on up the mountain, got on out there to the house. Carl just kept pouring the liquor in him. I said, "Carl, I'll be goddamn if you don't aim to get drunk."

"No," Carl says, "I'll not."

Boy, he got so drunk it was a sight on earth! We come on home, but he fell off the mule a time or two.

This story illustrates how easy it was to get whiskey from the Hardcastles, especially when one befriended them. It also tells something of the influence that easy whiskey had on the men of the community. More than anything else, however, the narrative explains why the Hardcastles had a shoot-out with the sheriff's posse east of Jessetown not long afterward. Tault Hardcastle, feeling that his federal license should be honored by local officials, was chafed from having to haul his cargo of legal whiskey by the back roads. He resolved that it was time to take the main road to Tall Rock by way of Jessetown. The test came in September 1916, when another shipment of bonded whiskey he had ordered was scheduled to arrive by rail east of Jessetown.

Accustomed as they were to having things their way in Owenton County, the Hardcastles made a big to-do of the coming event. Tault and Balm Hardcastle were to make the trip, along with Tault's wife Fannie, her brother Chester Beary, and a young hired hand, Schuyler Dark. Their job was to guard the whiskey and see to it that it did not fall into the hands of local law officials. They sent word to Jes "Black Socks" Birmingham, the Fountain County sheriff, not to interfere with their passage through his county and the county seat at Jessetown. According to an eyewitness to the subsequent events, whose description appeared in a Jessetown paper in later years, the Hardcastles boasted that this time they were "going through Jessetown or going to hell." Jessetown at that time was like the rest of Tennessee—bone dry.

Sheriff Birmingham returned word to the Hardcastles to bring along their caskets if they insisted on going through with their plans. He organized a posse of eight or nine men and deployed them on the Carpley road at the Jessetown city limits. They would ambush the Hardcastle party! In the meantime, the eyewitness quoted above had remained in town. He described the situation there as tense and highly uneasy, then proceeded to tell about the ambush itself:

As soon as possible I rushed over in town to find men standing around in small groups talking about what might happen if the sheriff didn't stop them. The one bank was closed, all stores were closed, and every one was very tense, as the Hardcastle gang was known as a very tough bunch and some expected that if they weren't stopped they might burn the town down. . . .

Well, I, along with about a half-dozen others my age, volunteered to take the message to the sheriff. But we only got three or four blocks on the way until there was only one with me. . . . He and I found the posse sooner than I expected, pretty well concealed on the north side of the Carpley road. . . . It was just a few minutes after we gave the sheriff the message that we heard the wagon approaching from the east. . . . Just as the wagon was opposite the sheriff who was about ten feet from the road, the sheriff called "halt" twice in a loud distinct voice. A man on the right rear of the wagon whirled and fired a rifle at the sheriff at what was almost point-blank range. At about the same instant a woman seated next to the man stood up and started screaming. The sheriff emptied a double-barreled shotgun into the right side of Schuyler Dark's head. At that time shooting became general. The woman was struck in the head by 17 buckshot. She fell out into the road along with her brother, who had been seated on the left rear of the wagon on the cases of Old Crow whiskey. The woman was dead instantly, and her brother had many wounds but none fatal.

The mules pulling the wagon never stopped. It was about this time that I observed a man on the front seat of the wagon reach under his shirt and come out with a pistol and turn in his seat and fire three times back toward the posse. There was so much sounds from the posse's guns that the only way one could determine this was by the recoil of the gun and a puff of smoke from the muzzle. In the meantime the mules were going along at about their normal pace. Birmingham had walked out into the road and was exchanging shot for shot with someone out of sight. Several members of the posse started running away, and I called and asked them where they were going, and they replied that their guns were empty. I reminded them that they could load moving toward the sheriff as well as the other way, that the sheriff was apt to get killed out in the road alone. After that everyone walked out into the road and started observing the dead woman and her wounded brother. It was about that time that some concealed person in the woods in the direction in which the two men had been

A family from Owenton County, Kentucky, near Tall Rock, 1924. The young man at bottom right vied for leadership among the area's moonshiners with the passing of the Hardcastle whiskey kingdom. His brother, second from top right, shared numerous memories of the area's history.

riding the front of the wagon fired a shot over our heads. That was the instant that I decided that I had seen and heard enough for one Saturday afternoon, so I plunged into the woods on the south side and kept on running until I came out on the road.

The Hardcastle dead were Schuyler Dark and Fannie Hardcastle. Young Dark, even after sustaining a bullet wound to the head, had propped himself up on an elbow and continued to shoot his Winchester until he died. It was said that a tooth, ripped from his mouth when he was shot, was saved and presented to his uncle, Art Baylanch, who carried it in his pocketbook for years after the ambush. Dark's and Fannie's bodies were taken to Jessetown for burial preparation.

Fannie was the daughter of Fil and Lotta Beary, and Tault Hardcastle's wife of only a few months. She was well into pregnancy when she made this fateful trip with her husband. The buckshot struck her about the face and head, and Fannie died instantly, falling head first from the wagon into the road. Her brother, Chester Beary, mourned her death for the rest of his life, grieving that "when they killed her, they killed her baby, too." Her body was laid out on a table in the Fountain County courthouse to be dressed for burial. She had been attired in a man's coat and hat at the time of her death, perhaps as an intended disguise.

Wounded members of the Hardcastle party included Chester Beary and both Balm and Tault Hardcastle. Balm was injured slightly in the foot but managed to elude the law and traverse the 10 to 15 miles of rugged terrain between there and his home at Tall Rock. A neighbor recalled seeing Balm Hardcastle the next morning at the end of the laborious trip, and of bidding goodbye to him for the last time.

We were sitting there talking, and heard an old hound barking way up on the mountain—moaning. Balm said, "I guess I'd better go. That might be the bloodhounds right now coming after me. I'd better make it over the state line." We didn't live far from the state line—about a mile. He went and got him something to eat, and went off walking up the hill. I was there with him, just a boy. He was eating as he walked along. I never did see him no more. I reckon he moved to Illinois or somewhere up north.

The previously quoted eyewitness to the ambush told what happened to Tault after he was wounded: "He was hit and unable to travel. That night he got cold and built a fire, but when the fire got out of control, he was not able to get away from the heat and began calling for help. Everyone was afraid to go to him, as he was heavily armed." Fannie's mother, Lotta Beary, told a narrator "that she got the word and got on a horse [20 miles to the north] and come out to where the trouble was that night. She said Tault was hid down behind some logs, and people was afraid to go to him. And she said she called to him when she got there and told him who she was. She went to him. He was shot up pretty bad. Said a piece of his underwear had went into his lungs." Lotta emerged with Tault's guns, and he was carried out on a stretcher and taken to the Fountain

County jail, where his brother-in-law, Chester Beary, was already lodged. Tault was never indicted for his actions that day.

It was not very long, perhaps no more than a week or so, before he married his third wife, Fannie's sister Inis Beary. From all indications, the marriage was motivated by fear and insecurity. Tault's past lay too heavy on him. His brother and wife (and some said his father and a heretofore unmentioned first wife as well) were dead at his hands or because of him. Another brother was still in prison for killing a man, and a third brother was gone from home for good. Tault's own future was uncertain, and his subsequent actions reflected an inability to cope with the situation. With his life and his whiskey empire in shambles, he sought refuge in Peoria, Illinois, in the company of his wife and children and her brother and sister-in-law.[4] During the intervening period, prior to their departure from Tall Rock, Tault never went anywhere without one of his children with him on the horse for bodily protection. Tault's paranoia finally killed him, according to a narrator who got her information from Claxton Hardcastle's widow. She said that Tault got into an altercation with his son-in-law in Illinois, was shot in the leg during the ensuing struggle, and died of fright: "He'd been shot up during the ambush out yonder and lived through it," she observed, "and when he was shot in the leg he just died."

When Tault moved from Tall Rock, he left behind memories of a whiskey kingdom that are yet to be forgotten. Between the years 1865 and 1935 a total of 126 indictments, mainly whiskey-related, were handed down by the Owenton County Circuit Court against members of the extended Hardcastle family. Of that number, 86 were against either Tault or his brother Crane. Tault was charged 55 times in 1916 alone.[5] Tim Roberts and Trunk Westmorlans along with two or three others in the Tall Rock area, vied for leadership among the bootleggers for the next 40 years, but their names were never comparable to that of Hardcastle. With the Hardcastles gone, big-time bootlegging passed from the State Line country.

A Changing Culture

THE 33 KILLINGS that took place between 1915 and 1940 marked a dramatic increase in the local homicide rate. Such a prolific demonstration of violence reflects a basic alteration of the area's social and economic structure, which was brought about chiefly by the introduction of extractive industry and the new reality of wage employment. To obtain a fuller perspective on the violent episodes that occurred mainly during the period between the two world wars, it should be helpful to examine both the static and dynamic character of State Line economy for those trying years. The killings themselves will be described in the next chapter.

Families in the study area during those years were sustained by farming, moonshining, logging and sawmilling activities, or some combination of the three. Agriculture remained the most important, however, as self-sufficient farming was the cornerstone of their way of life, providing adequately for landowners and tenant farmers alike. Only a very few less fortunate families, headed by individuals who reportedly were so lazy that they would rather steal and beg than do a day's work, fell outside the bounds of this venerated economic system, which spelled out a life that was generally satisfying even though devoid of frills. People here shared a commitment to the land, however eroded and thin and rocky its soil, and they depended on it for their very existence. Their marginal self-sufficiency was based on the premise that a single nuclear family, laboring together, could generally depend on the land for food, clothing, shelter, and many forms of recreation as well. Even the bit of extra income that most families derived from outside sources each year came from the land in the form of a cash crop: tobacco, dried fruits, a few head of hogs and cattle, wild animal hides, and medicinal plants like ginseng and yellowroot.

The typical farm of the between-the-wars era consisted of a little bottomland, devoted mainly to corn and small grains, and lower mountain slopes that had been cleared for hay and pasture. Steeper cleared areas were used almost exclusively for noncultivated pastureland and fruit trees. Edible wild game was plentiful; wild berries and nuts, available everywhere, were gathered by the boys and girls to help supplement the family's winter food supply.

Mechanization in agricultural practices was slow in coming, as money was in extremely short supply. While a limited number of farms had tractors with steel cleats by the 1930s, most boasted no machines beyond horse-drawn plows, cultivators, mowing machines, and hay rakes—all more frequently in a state of disrepair than in service. Scythes, cradles, flailing sticks, wooden harrows, hoes, and other small hand tools were much in evidence as functioning relics of the nineteenth century. For families residing in the valleys, the day had passed when row crops were planted entirely by hand, but people at the heads of the small hollows and on Rutherford Mountain still lived much like their preindustrial ancestors. The soil in these upland areas was thin and often too rocky for plows. Three persons recalled without any show of fond remembrance what it was like to plant, cultivate, and harvest corn under such adverse circumstances:

The ground was rocky. All of it couldn't be plowed with a double shovel. They had to plow it with a bull-tongue plow, for with a double-shovel plow rocks would hang in between the plows, and you'd have to stop and get them loose. But a bull-tongue plow would work its way right through the rocks. I've seen Tony Stanley plowing over yonder on that hillside with a bull-tongue plow. And he'd run right under them rocks with that plow and them rocks would roll off over the hill and tear down several stalks of corn as they went.

They'd plant corn by laying off the rows by hand, and then by dropping the corn and covering it with hoes. You'd just have to get the rocks out of the way with the hoe.

Old Man Tony Kenner lived close to my daddy. And they'd get their crops planted, you know. My daddy had a little grist mill that he'd grind corn meal with. And Old Man Tony come down there to the mill. Dad says, "How does your corn look?"

"Well, I God," he said, "you can get out early of a morning when the dew is on it, part the weeds, and look down at it," says, "it looks pert!"

Another old man there tried to raise corn on them old mountain fields. It wouldn't make nothing. Corn would just get up as high as your knee and just dry up. Jes McKinley told him, "Get you a big long plow and make three furrows to the row. That'll make it come out and it'll make good corn."

Well, he went to the blacksmith shop and put three bull-tongue plows together to make three furrows to the row. Well, he ran that through the rows and said that the plants just wilted down behind him. It didn't make nary thing. Said, "Don't pay no attention to that Jes McKinley. That'll ruin your corn every time."

The bench I lived on was rocky. It was so rocky, in some places where we tended corn I'd take a hoe and we'd walk and hunt a place where we could get some loose dirt—two, three, five feet away. Then we walked back over here and covered up the grains of corn with the dirt. Drop the corn into the opening between the rocks, then bring the dirt and cover it up. I wore out a hoe every three years in that sandstone soil. We used a bull-tongue plow when we could, but in some places the rock was so bad that the plow would just turn the rock over, and the rock would fall right back in the same place.

The last narrator said in an absolute way that the rocks in the upland areas were an ever-present source of aggravation. The tone of his voice verged on bitterness, reflecting a resentment against his early physical and cultural environment. Such sentiments explain, in part at least, why he and others around him grew up to be a part of the troublemaking element. He ended the subject by expressing his attitude toward life in general: "I learned that anything I wanted I had to work hard for, and I wasn't going to let anyone take it away from me."

Still another narrator to address the subject of the poor, rocky soil recalled that members of a hard-up Owenton County

Outcroppings of resistant rock formations dominate the State Line country. This one is in Brake County, Kentucky, near the Waterfall community.

family in the Tall Rock vicinity "pulled grapevines in the mountains to feed their horse at dinner [noon]." He then continued, "Why, they couldn't make enough corn! I don't reckon they made more than enough corn to do for the family. I recall, too, used to we'd grow a little redtop clover for hay. But it would take five acres to make enough of it to winter a goose!"

An unemployed former bootlegger who had grown up on the short side of plenty, and whose standard of living is still extremely lean, recalled going hungry during the early 1930s: "Back then it was hard to make a living. Now the truth don't hurt nobody. I've got up a many a day and went out to look for work without a bite of breakfast or a bite to eat in the house. When we got some money [at the end of the day], we'd go by a store and buy it up in grub and take it home and eat it. Lot of people wouldn't want to own up to it, but we was raised up hard."

Such descriptions implied far more than these peoople spoke regarding basic attitudes and what they expected from life. After hearing such accounts, one is not hard put to understand the introduction and presence of a moonshining culture, and perhaps the existence and acceptance of violence as a way of life. The narrators never complained of their estate in life in earlier years, but they never apologized for their own actions or those of their people during the hard times. These families were poor at that time, even by their own standards. They subsisted mainly on foods with high starch and grease content. Typically the diet consisted of "cornbread, middling meat, meal gravy, and coffee for breakfast. Maybe a little milk. But they didn't have very much milk. Now they ate that a lot; had it three meals a day." One of the most poignant pre-Depression recollections recorded was a female narrator's response when asked whether she experienced periods of hunger as a child in the 1920s. She stared into space for a long moment and then replied: "Yes, many a time. They was eight of us kids in the family, plus our parents. And some mornings we just had enough meal in the house to make one hoecake, you know, on top of the stove. And we had to divide that ten ways." In a voice filled with emotion, this woman, who appeared to be little better off today, concluded, "Now that was our breakfast."

Starches, carbohydrates, and fats were relied on extensively, especially during winter months. It appears that the ever-present cornbread, biscuits, gravy, fried potatoes, and dried beans, with few or no fresh fruits and vegetables, resulted in "colds and runny noses all the time in wintertime" for children and adults alike. One narrator, who included himself among the have-nots, related a humorous anecdote illustrating the almost total reliance on bread among Rutherford Mountain families:

Tony Janis lived up there close to us. My daddy and Tony growed wheat that year. They went and had some ground [into flour].

Tony had a big old boy called Lawson. Tony come back (and his wife was Fronie), and he went to breakfast and Lawson was a-crying. Tony said, "Fronie, can you tell me what Lawson is crying about?"

"Well," she said, "Tony, I'll just tell you, he's wanting some bread to eat with his biscuits!" [Heavy laughter]

The main difference in the wintertime diets of the various families was that the poorer ones typically had no adequate supply of dried and canned fruits and vegetables to turn to as a healthful means of diversifying the menu. By way of comparison, it was not uncommon for women whose family incomes allowed them to purchase the necessary jars, sugars, and spices to preserve between 300 and 450 quart and half-gallon glass jars of fruits and vegetables for storage in neat rows in the cellar, or for the same families to produce large quantities of turnips, cabbage, apples, and potatoes for bulk storage in cellars and earthen pits.

By 1915, most of the families in the valley areas were living in frame or board-over-log houses, generally painted white. Bare exterior logs were still much in evidence on Rutherford Mountain structures, however. And regardless of their geographical location or building materials, all dwellings in the study area shared a common characteristic—cold interiors during winter months, especially after stove or fireplace flames died down at night. The finer details of construction had been omitted in most of the houses: it was not uncommon for a "nice frame house" to have one-inch cracks under the outside doors and windows that let the wind in around the casings. It takes little imagination, then, to figure out how much cold air entered the log cabins through their puncheon floors and poorly chinked log walls. Numerous people told of awakening on frigid mornings to find their beds covered with a blanket of snow that had been forced through the cracks in the wall by strong winds.

Although agriculture remained paramount during the period, some families resorted to making or continued to make illegal whiskey as a means of surviving the 1920s and 1930s. "Back then," recalled one narrator, "they's a lot of people in the country that made liquor; had to to survive. It was corn whiskey—straight corn." Whiskey provided the only source of cash income for certain mountain and valley landowners, and for some landless, indigent tenant farmers as well. One person from the unskilled tenant class readily admitted to making whiskey: "Now the truth don't hurt nobody. I made whiskey myself years ago, and I've sold it, plenty of it." But he made a critical distinction between the older and newer whiskey—a distinction verified by others. "This was sugar whiskey that I made," he said. "I've heard of corn whiskey, but it was just too much time and trouble to fool with. You could take a barrel of mash and not get enough straight whiskey to pay you to fool with it. You couldn't get more than a gallon and three quarts from a 60-gallon barrel." A former sheriff corroborated the statement: "Sugared whiskey turns out more whiskey. If you· don't sugar so heavy, you don't have the headache, but you don't have as much whiskey. And the more sugar, the worse the hangover." After about 1920, demand for liquor on short notice and in abundance, brought about by changing lifestyles, sounded the death knell for old-time corn liquor.

Local society at all levels continued to condone the practice of making and selling illegal whiskey as perhaps an outright necessity for most of those persons involved. No one sanctioned the use of inadequate equipment or ignorance of the brewing process, however, as either instance often produced poisoned whiskey and left behind a trail of tragedy in sickness, accidental death, and sometimes retributive killing. One person charged that some of the moonshiners were either ignorant or immoral, or both. "Some of the ones that made whiskey put buckeye or lye or laurel [poisonous ingredients] in it to make it bead," he stated rather bluntly. "It would just bead away, but it wudn't worth nothing. It was poisoned and would kill you. . . . They'd take it out to the railroad tracks [in the sawmilling camps] and sell it to anybody they could."

Many families made and sold illegal whiskey. Available court records and oral traditions in the four counties collectively identified at least 25 separate State Line families from which one or more members, including women, were indicted for trafficking in moonshine. It was not always easy to get convictions against them, however, as merchants and businessmen in the county seat towns relied on these sources for their own whiskey, and would speak favorably of the moonshiners to court officials.

While every locality had its small moonshining enterprises,

The fellow on the left, in this photo from the 1920s, grew up at the foot of Tall Rock at the head of Honey Creek and befriended moonshiner and lawman alike. He recalled numerous violent episodes that took place in the locality.

the bigger whiskey-making operations continued to be identified with Tall Rock, even after the Hardcastles had passed from the scene. The major activity there from the 1920s into the 1950s involved four names: Tim Roberts, Trunk Westmorlans, "Speedy" Christie, and the Tarters. Revenue men, accompanied by Owenton and Trundle County law officers, frequently staged raids and made arrests of these individuals as well as such smaller bootleggers in the area as the Talbots, Husteds, Lyonses, Wells, and Slaytons. In Brake County, on the other hand, law enforcement officials had their hands full with the Coffelts, Statons, Baylanches, Langnesses, and others who operated between Waterfall and Mt. Gilead. One narrator, who lived on upper Honey Creek near Rutherford Mountain, provided an indication of how prolific the moonshine stills were on the mountain during those years on both sides of the state line:

We used to run cattle and hogs back there on the mountain. We'd run them out there winter and summer. We had seven to eight old sows that stayed back there all the time. They's making liquor back there, plenty of it. One morning I went back to see the hogs and cattle, to salt them or something. I went back there on a horse that morning. They'd go to their stills—the old sows would—and drink that slop. The hogs had bells on. Well, I run up on five stills that morning, and every one of them was working—a-doubling. At one place, they's two stills at the same place. I knew whose they were. I'd stop and fill up with liquor, too. [Laughter]

That same narrator, whose home was close to Tall Rock, was frequently in a position to warn the moonshiners there of the approach of lawmen on a raiding mission, as the following story illustrates. It also demonstrates how local sheriffs were often forced by federal authorities into the unpleasant task of raiding the whiskey-making operations of their friends and neighbors:

Dad owned a place up there close to Tall Rock. Well, he owned two or three places up there. One had a good peach orchard on it, and they sent me up there one day to get some peaches. I got on the horse and went up there and got the peaches, and come back down by a fellow's house. I stopped to get me some liquor.

I got some, and he had some good peach brandy. I got a half-gallon of it and just tied it to the slicker on my horse. Come on down, and met the law going up—revenue. I heard somebody talking back behind me and I's a-looking back, and my horse was just a-trotting on down the road. Then all at once the horse stopped. I looked around and there's Finley Crutchfield, the sheriff out there at Worley, and two or three more. I didn't know them. I said, "What are you doing?"

He had hold of my horse's bridle. He said, "You like to have rode over me."

I said, "I was a-looking back and didn't see you." He talked awhile, and this revenue man started to lay his hand up on my saddle there where that liquor was. I just turned my side, throwed my leg back out that way, and he took hold of my leg. Come on down the road, and they went on. Well, this revenue man was looking straight at that liquor, too. But Finley didn't pay no attention to it.

I came on just a little further and met my dad and Hascal Crutchfield [Finley's father]. He was sheriff over here in Trundle. I said, "Finley up there like to have scared me to death a while ago."

Hascal said, What?"

I said, "He stopped my horse," and I said, "I was afraid he was going to search me."

Hascal said, "Did you have any liquor?"

I said, "Yeah, got a half-gallon here." I said, "Do you want a drink?"

Hascal says, "No, I don't want none." Says, "I want it, but that there fool Boles [revenue man], if he was to smell it on me, he'd tell it everywhere." He said, "Did you get that from Trunk Westmorlans up here?"

I said, "Yeah."

And he said, "That's where they're going right now, to search the house. Does he have some more whiskey?"

I says, "Yeah, I guess he has. I don't know. He just went in the smokehouse and got it. I just walked out and came on down the hill." I said, "I guess he's got it."

"Well," he says, "they're going to search him. Finley is going up there to search him—him and Boles, this revenue man." Says, "Can you get back up through that-a-way and get there and tell him?"

I says, "No, I can't."

"Well," he says, "I'll tell you what I'll do." Says, "His brother-in-law's right down here on a wagon." Says, "You go down there and tell him to take one of his mules out and go up the road here, go around us, and I'll slow them down up here." Says, "They're going to wait for me, and I'll slow them down until he can get up there and tell Trunk."

Well, I went on down there and told Sandusky about it. Sandusky took out one of his mules and went around the road, went up there and told Trunk. Old Trunk says, "I'd better get my liquor out." And he run in to get the liquor. It was in their saddle pockets. He come out and started off over the hill, Shirley [Sandusky] said. And Trunk hadn't got down the hill [until he remembered that he] had forgot to give Shirley a drink [as a reward for warning him], and he turned around and come back to the house to give him a drink of liquor! And the law got him!

I come on down that day after Finley stopped me up there. Come on down to Uncle Ben Emory's store. I told Uncle Ben, I says, "That there Finley like to have scared me to death up there awhile ago." I said, "I thought he was going to search me." And I said, "I want to put my liquor here in the store."

Uncle Ben said, "Hell, no, you don't put it in the store!" Says, "Take it down there in the field and put it in the bottom of the corn shock." I did. Well, Hascal and my dad come on back down and they's acting the fool there. The law had Trunk, and I have forgot how many gallons of liquor. They set it down there. Hascal told me, said, "Whose is that liquor there?"

I said, "Finley will get after me [if I tell]."

"No, he won't. Go and get it."

Finley says, "No, help yourself to it." I opened a can of liquor. . . . Hascal said, "You better be careful or I'll go out there and search the slicker on your saddle."

I said [chuckling], "Go ahead." I'd done took it out, you know, took it on down there in the field. "Go ahead and search me."

Trunk Westmorlans was sent to prison for this violation, and for other infractions as well. He was not alone in being indicted on moonshining charges, however, as a number of his business rivals were charged, convicted, and sentenced to prison on numerous occasions.

Illegal whiskey-making intensified during the 1930s, 1940s, and well into the 1950s. Because of stepped-up law enforcement the practice slowed down with the passing of that generation but reputedly has not entirely died out in the area yet. While these men cannot be unduly condemned for providing

A small sawmilling operation in Brake County, Kentucky, c. 1910. *Below*, loggers from Lightsboro, Kentucky, pose with their sweethearts in 1926.

for their families by making and selling whiskey during those trying years, the ease with which the product could be obtained was a chief factor in some of the area's homicides.

The timber industry constituted the third chief enterprise in the area's tripartite economy from about 1915 to 1940. On its western margin, the eastern hardwood forest extends into the State Line country, which was one time covered densely in virgin timber. The steeper interior slopes retained their wealth of fine trees until around 1915, when the large oak, chestnut, yellow poplar, walnut, cherry, pine, and cedar fell under the saws of local logging crews sent into the woods by the big commercial sawmilling companies that had finally penetrated this portion of the Upper South. Their logging and lumbering operations crawled along the ridges and up the streams and hollows until, by the mid-1930s, every foot of land had been logged and stripped by this invasion of the Appalachian lumber barons, who had operated in other parts of the region for at least 25 years.

All of the modern mills that were introduced into the area by the large exploitative companies were bandmills, whose saw blades operate as a continuous steel belt on movable frames. "Logs were pulled into place on a carriage by means of a pulley, and they would shoot through them logs just like a rifle gun," explained one narrator. The first bandmill in the study area was the Whitley mill, established in 1914 or 1915 in Brake County at the head of Rocky Valley, about a mile north of the state line. The Tennessee Stave and Lumber Company, with headquarters in Cincinnati, moved about that same time into the area at the head of the Grand Forks of the Bear River and began cutting timber from several thousand acres of land, assisted by local subcontractors who negotiated with the parent company to cut the trees and delivered the logs to a mill located at the head of the main prong of the Bear.

Ohio-born O.R. Abraham, who had moved to Jessetown in the early 1900s because of the area's excellent stands of timber, gained timber rights to thousands of acres in and east of Buffalo Lick Hollow through his negotiations with the small farmer/hunters who owned the land. Most of his lumbering occurred from the late 1920s to the mid-1930s, although his sawmilling ventures weathered the Great Depression and persisted into the post–World War II era.

East of the Whitley operation and north of the Tennessee Stave and the Abraham holdings was the Stearns Coal and Lumber Company, the only one still in operation in the study area. That company currently owns the land (and mineral rights) once logged over by the other three companies. When Stearns came into possession of Tennessee Stave and Lumber in the mid-1920s, it accelerated efforts to build narrow-gauge railroad tracks up every hollow and along every ridge to facilitate logging operations on both sides of the state line. Today, however, the Stearns mills in the study area are silent; the company has leased timber rights to smaller operators, who continue to log the area.

The exploitation of local timber resources—concurrent with limited drilling for oil and gas—resulted in the introduction of twentieth-century economic standards into an area of previously self-sufficient households. For the first time, wage employment on a grand scale was available to local men whose daily routines had consisted mainly of walking behind a team of mules as they laboriously pulled a turning plow or a row cultivator through small red clay fields that contained more rocks than dirt, more gullies than level land.

Logging and sawmilling activities employed hundreds of people. To say that an average of one man per family worked in the lumber industry would be understating the new employment situation. Each of the big commercial mills hired between 50 and 70 men, including a superintendent, foreman, bookkeeper, sawyers, saw filers, log jackers (men who positioned the logs on the moving carriage for sawing), edgers (those who squared the planks and knocked off the residual bark), off bearers (who carried the planks from the mill to the stackers), slab carriers, lumber stackers, and dust monkeys (young boys who carted the sawdust out of the large hole below the saw blade "and come a-running back to get another'n").

Additionally, the logging subcontractors employed their own crews of 18 to 30 men.

The true extent of logging and milling accidents will never be known, as the companies kept no records of this sort, and hospitalization insurance and workmen's compensation were unheard of in the mountains. The only records of the accidents are oral, and many of the men who worked in the timber industry during those early years are gone. Nevertheless, I recorded oral descriptions in an effort to get at the frequent episodes of violence and death these men witnessed, episodes that helped to shape their perceptions of the lethal interpersonal violence that occurred all around them in the logging camps. Most narratives about death in the woods were vivid and lucid, as seen in the following account of a fatal accident in the early 1920s:

> I was cutting timber for Ernie Boyer back here on the Barkwell farm up on Sapling Mountain [in southern Brake County]. Me and Hank McKinley and Oren Bale was working together. They was another crew working on around to the left of us. And what happened there, there was a red oak about 18 inches through at the bottom, and we notched it and sawed it down.
>
> Well, they was a dead chestnut that stood right straight back behind it. But we watched that dead chestnut the best we could. And if the oak ever shook a limb when it touched the tree, we didn't know it. Well, the tree fell. I got my axe and measuring stick and I walked out on the other side of the log and measured off a 14-foot log. And Oren Bale just picked up the crosscut saw and come around on the lower side. And they was a dead limb on his side. He said, "If you'll give me the axe, I'll cut this limb and you won't have to cross the log."
>
> Well, by the time I went to reach him the axe, Hank McKinley—he was helping Oren saw, was humped over there to cut the limb. That chestnut come down and hit him right across the head. It just mashed the who-o-o-le top of his head in. Just knocked him on his hunkers. He never did speak or nothing. He lived, I guess, about 30 minutes.

These woodsmen never complained about working conditions or wages, as they felt that the nature of the job had a built-in risk factor and that in spite of the danger involved, they were well paid for their labors, especially compared with what a

Three farmer-sawmill workers from Honey Creek, Tennessee, in the
early 1930s.

man could get for a day's work as a farm laborer. Farmhands were typically paid 50 cents a day, plus lunch; early timber cutters and mill workers received at least $1.50 daily, and by the mid-1920s some of them earned upward of $3.00 for a day's work.

The ages of the woodsmen ranged from the very old—those who did little more than piddle around the camps at odd jobs, such as keeping the ox and mule stalls clean—to the extremely young, like the 14-year-olds who worked as dust monkeys. By and large, however, the male population of the sawmilling camps was made up of young family men and perhaps still younger single fellows, all of whom were there to get their share of the new money that was being flashed around. Whatever the age, most of these men were away from home and a self-sufficient family enterprise for the first time. Some lived as far as 15 miles from their places of employment, and they rode horseback or walked the round trip each day. They were already tired when they got to work and exhausted before they got home; morning came all too early. For many of the men, a live-in arrangement seemed more feasible and certainly easier on their bodies.

Some stayed in nearby caves, as one man explained:

I've cut timber all over this Gilead country. And we'd box us up a rock house [bluff] and stay in it winter and summer. They'd generally be about six of us. Every Friday evening we'd leave there and come home to Hat Hollow.

We had to do all our cooking back there. It wasn't fit for a dog to eat, but we ate it. For breakfast, we'd have meat and eggs and make us up a flapjack, pour it in a pan, and turn it over and cook it. Sometimes we'd have about six or seven of them stacked up. We'd bake cornbread for dinner, take it to the woods with us. Come back that night and cook again.

We took quilts from home to sleep on in the rock house shelter. Slept on the ground. We burned green hickory poles and so on for heat in the winter. The smoke escaped by following the contour of the cliff [to the outside].

More of the men, however, boarded in homes located close to their work, others preferred to move into housing, however

This 1984 bluff-shelter home of a Trundle County recluse looks much like the ones occupied by area loggers between the world wars.

crude, provided by the employers in the logging and milling camps. The contractor for the Whitley mill in Rocky Valley built 35 to 40 cabins near his own home for his team drivers and some of the less important workers as well—crude "boxed, board and batten shacks, only one plank thick." Living in them, the narrators asserted, was "just like living out of doors; just like they was out in the weather." Winters in the area sometimes brought up to 30 inches of snow and temperatures that frequently dipped below zero.

The Whitley camp experienced epidemics of whooping cough and measles that "killed two or three people a day at one time there. It was just like hauling a bunch of hogs [out of] there for a while." Doctors were brought in, but they were unable to stem the tide of death that the diseases produced. Reportedly, on one occasion there were "18 people took out of that camp one day that had died with the flu." Other camps, too, experienced sickness and death, but apparently nothing to compare with Whitley's. O.R. Abraham's camp in Buffalo Lick Hollow—with its seven houses for workers, a boardinghouse, and two barns—seemingly afforded a better quality of shelter for the occupants. Yet surprisingly, perhaps, the Abraham camp witnessed more than its share of killings.

Stearns Coal and Lumber Company, which also had milling operations in Buffalo Lick Hollow, contracted Garland Boyer to do its logging. His first cousins, Gary and Acie Boyer, logged in the adjacent Billings Creek locality for that same company. Actually, the three Boyers had started out together in the logging business but went separate ways when Garland and one of his cousins were unable to get along. Cap Washam and his wife kept Garland's boardinghouse and cooked the meals for the men, who lived nearby in railroad boxcars that had been brought in to serve as makeshift living quarters. These boxcars generally constituted satisfactory housing for the men and their families, as their tongue-and-groove construction made them airtight. Garland Boyer himself lived in camp during the week but never consented to bring his wife and children there. His widow, 94 years old in 1985, provided a written description of life and work in the camp:

Garland Boyer run a logging job for Stearns Coal and Lumber Co. in 1924-25 and part of '26. He hired men to work from the surrounding community. He also run a boardinghouse—usually a husband and wife. The man worked in the woods, the woman to cook for the workers (with someone to help her). The workers cut the trees. Sawed the logs with crosscut saws. Dragged (they called it skidding) the logs by mules to a location where they could be picked up by the company's train. Boyer kept about 20 mules on the job. The wages was from $1 to $1.50 per day. The workers would go home over the weekend, then come back on Sunday evening for work on Monday. Only one family lived there all the time. The food was mostly beans, kraut, potatoes, cornbread, meat. And for breakfast, biscuit, ham, sausage, and molasses for sweets. I never heard of anyone grumbling about the food. After work the men would play games with cards for fun. No drinking or gambling for money was allowed on the job. There was more men worked some days than others. Never any regular number. Most was married, and of different ages. A few was single, and slept and eat at the boarding-house. No woman lived in camp, except those who run the boardinghouse, and one family, Cap and Susie Ragsdale and three children, lived on the job.

The fact that workers who lived on the job site included married as well as single men accounts for much of the violence that gripped every camp on several occasions. If meals were often inadequate at home (depending on the season of the year), they were disastrous for men trying to cook for themselves. Initial feelings of loneliness and homesickness grew into tensions that, coupled with the whiskey readily available everywhere, were often manifested in loud, uninhibited voices and disorderly actions. The presence of women in the camps, whether wives, daughters, or "loose women" who drifted in and out and "weren't worth fighting over," made matters even worse. Drunken brawls, lovers' quarrels, fights between rivals for a woman's affections, and gambling with dice and cards all made the flourishing of knives or guns a commonplace occurrence. Several killings took place under these conditions (one narrator exaggerated the number at "two or three killings a week"); acts of lesser violence were so numerous as to make all efforts to catalog them fruitless. It was not at all surprising to learn that after two years of employment in the woods, one narrator quit his job and moved to Cincinnati. When asked why he chose to give up a job near home that paid 30 cents an hour for a city job in a roofing factory that paid exactly the same, he responded emphatically, "I just wanted to get out of that mess. I'd had all I wanted."

Although the four largest sawmilling companies employed countless men from the area during the 1920s and '30s, there is no indication that they underpaid their employees or mistreated them in other ways. The killings that took place in the camps and in the woods were motivated by very personal concerns. In fact, although the timber industry in the State Line country created frictions between old and new ways of living that often resulted in homicides, the greatest social conflicts of all came with the departure of the big sawmills from the area as a result of the Great Depression. The woodsmen, who had continually shifted in and out of employment at the mills, went home in despair when the lumbering operations ended.

The logging camps and mills did nothing to influence the general social development of the area, since the energies of the lumber companies were concentrated on the removal of timber, not on the restoration of the land or its human resources. "After the Whitley mill closed in the 1920s," one narrator noted, "the people did just the best they could; just worked harder here and yonder when they could get a day's work on the farm or something like that." He then added in a voice that seemed preoccupied with memories of bad times, "I'm telling you, it was hard going."

Many of the former timbermen roamed the countryside looking for work but seldom found it. They tried as best they could to support their families, but were only marginally successful in this regard. Women and children, too, joined in the efforts to find occasional farm labor and domestic employment, but their efforts did little to alleviate the effects of the Great Depression that by then could be seen all around them.

One should not be surprised at the large volume of moonshine that was made, sold, and consumed during the 1920s and 1930s, as these two decades were in all likelihood the hardest ever experienced by people in the State Line country. Unrestrained actions and killings kept pace with the social tensions produced by the coming of the sawmills and, subsequently, with the economic ills that resulted from their leaving. The unpleasant consequences are described in the next chapter.

4

Violence between the World Wars

THE EASE with which whiskey could be obtained taught the residents of the State Line country to accept drinking, brawling, knifing, and gunshooting as common occurrences. The death of a close relative in a drunken brawl was an ever-present possibility and became reality all too often. A former sheriff testified that "90 percent or more of the knifings and shootings in that area were alcohol related. Someone would get into an argument about something when they're drinking, and that generally led up to a killing." It was not the presence of whiskey that brought about the practice of carrying knives and guns as lethal weapons, however. The men of the study area had apparently done that for some time; the ready availability of alcohol simply intensified the practice. Between 1920 and 1940, every male who could afford a gun carried one at all times—typically, concealed—in the field, in the woods, at church, to the local store, and in town. (Even many teenage boys had guns, which they kept hidden from their parents.) They used the weapons both for protection from snakes and animals and for shooting their way "out of scrapes."

The testimony of several gunowners revealed insights into the gun culture of the State Line country. One person remembered that his first gun was a .45 Colt automatic for which he paid $18 and that he and his landlord often engaged in shooting matches in order to stay in good practice. He carried the gun between his underwear and shirt, tucked beneath the belt.

It was his constant companion, "especially when cutting timber" for the Tennessee Stave and Lumber Company in Buffalo Lick Hollow. "I felt mighty good with a gun on me," he reflected, "not to hurt anyone, but to defend myself." He went on to recall an occasion when he thought that his life would depend on using the gun.

I was going along one time and I seen a bunch of roughnecks out in front of me. I was riding a horse. I'd been over here to see her [his wife]. I was riding down Honey Creek, and they's a bunch of roughnecks out in front of me. I think to myself, "Now I'll have it out with them." And I had my hand in my coat pocket. And I decided not to try to jerk it out, just to keep it there, and if I had to shoot, to shoot from the pocket.

Went on up to them, and they was the friendliest bunch of people you've ever seen. Made me ashamed of myself. . . . They was a rough bunch ordinarily. But they wasn't drinking then like they usually did.

That same narrator also told of the time when, as a teenager, he borrowed a gun to carry to church as protection against a fellow who had threatened to run him off if he showed up. "I put the gun in my coat pocket," he remembered, "and when I got there I hung my coat up against the wall and that gun hit the wall just like a rock. I never was so ashamed of anything in my life."

In answer to the question as to why people in the sawmilling camps were so "rough" (a term he had used), another narrator responded emphatically, "Because everyone carried guns and they would use them! They were like pistols with the trigger filed down." Another person present volunteered the information that he personally "got a corn" on his shoulder from carrying a pistol in a shoulder holster. "That way," he said, "you could carry a big old long gun down in your sleeve and nobody could see it. I carried it all the time that I was running hogs in the woods with my daddy. I don't know why we carried them but everybody did it. We all had guns in the mountains."

If these fellows did not know why they carried guns (as several testified), they were all the more likely to use them at the drop of a hat if and when the occasion arose. They knew

Pistol-packing residents of the State Line country, 1929. More often, the guns were concealed.

what guns were for; their culture had taught them that. But without any sort of cultural prohibition against their use, guns were all too frequently wielded without any thought of the consequences. Once a gun (or knife) was out in the open, the owner's ego was at stake, leaving only one real course of action—to use the weapon in defense of personal honor. One narrator, whose boasting in the following account is reportedly typical of the life he lived, told of being shot in the leg by his cousin and of retaliating by shooting out his cousin's eye:

They was a whole bunch of my cousins that made liquor. They tried to run over me out there one day on the mountain. I had started into the Honey Creek country, over at Lank Hilham's. I had my shotgun with me. "Boom," went a shotgun and shot me right here in the leg. Well, boy, I shot him [Lugs Talbot] so quick, though, you couldn't have said, "Don't do that," until I had done shot him.

That went on for a long time. Finally, I met him in the road. I didn't care in that day and time. If he'd said anything to me, I'd a-grabbed him and th' owed it to him.

I'd pick up a man and throw him over my head just like I would a baby.

I met him in the road. See, his eye was out. I said, "What's the matter with you? Looks like you ain't got but one eye."

"Oh," he says, "some man shot me." He told me where it was at.

I said, "Let me tell you somethng. I'm the very one you shot, and I sure shot you, too, didn't I?"

"Oh," he said, "if I had knowed that was you, I wouldn't shot you for nothing in the world."

I said, "You'd better get you a gun before you shoot anybody else."

He said, "I thought I'd shoot that man and cripple him, then I was going to run up there and kill him and put him behind that big log."

I said, "Well, you'd better get a gun before you try another one." He was going to kill me so I couldn't catch them making liquor. He's up there at the road, watching, while the others made liquor. They's rough. They just believed in killing you. Everyone of Bull's boys was that way.

My field diary for March 8, 1984, contains a revealing entry about this narrator:

Since I arrived in Washington in the early afternoon, and since I was to pass by Perry Talbot's house at the edge of town, I decided to stop there first. He lived in a shelter that, at best, can be described as a shack. It was heated by a sheet metal stove with a hole burned through the side of it, and his little front room was so hot that I actually sat there and perspired from the intense heat (maybe it was due to my nervousness from being in his presence) as I talked with him. It didn't help matters any when he lifted a cushion on the sofa on which I sat to reveal a 9-shot, .22-caliber pistol. Thankfully, he didn't show me the gun as a show of force on his part. By that time, we were even on laughing terms, at least on occasion. He showed me the gun, it seems, to underscore the fact that he always carried a gun, and still does. He observed that he did so for protection. "You'd better have one if you want to live. Back then, I carried a .38 Special in a holster on my hip."

Perry was cooking cornbread in a black skillet on top of the stove. That's all the food that he had in the house, he told me; yet, he was going to share it with "the little birds" outside in the yard. I was touched with the tenderness exhibited by this man who literally wasn't afraid of anything or anybody.

A concomitant of whiskey consumption and carrying concealed deadly weapons was unrestrained behavior. Rowdiness had been common since about 1890 but seemingly grew worse during the period between the world wars. As noted earlier, much of this sort of behavior took place when these fellows got together in pairs and groups, especially at dances, outings, school functions, and church services. Some men of the community who were otherwise not inclined to violence, often carried guns to church and school activities to help guard against the unruly ones present: "I've known of Daddy many times taking his gun to church, you know. And there was an old rail fence, and he'd hide his gun in the fence and go on to church. After church, he'd go back and get it." One of the narrators was himself indicted in Brake County in May 1934, and fined $16.50 "for acting drunk, talking loud, and boisterous cursing and swearing, and for singing a very vulgar song at church at Rocky Valley." It is readily apparent from oral and printed sources that the congregation at Rocky Valley had its share of disturbance during the 1920s and '30s, as several additional warrants were sworn out for the arrests of the offenders. A resident of nearby Waterfall (a place that vied with Tall Rock for the reputation as the roughest locality in the State Line country), who was later killed in a gun battle between two families of close relatives, was indicted in October 1925 "for disturbing public worship by shooting guns and pistols into the church building and upon the church grounds."

Churches elsewhere in the study area also had incessant visitations from the hell-raising forces. The following account indicates the state of affairs on Bear River just before World War I:

> I was raised on Bear River, and they was some of the meanest people there that ever lived—the Majors, Carsons, the Odles, and the Bedes. And they was as mean as snakes. When Brother Robbins come in there to preach, he come past the store there with his guitar in his hand. And we was sitting on the store house porch there, and they made the remark, "We'll take that away from him and bust that baby over his head," and things like that.
>
> He went in there to the old Methodist Church at Bear River and went to preaching—went to holding a revival there, and that revival reformed that community, absolutely. They preached two hard weeks there. Brother Robbins would get out of the pulpit and go out in the yard and calm the fighting, and Sister Robbins would take the stand and go to preaching while he was out there.

The next description, shared by the narrator from Hat Hollow, reveals even more fully how rough and unmanageable the tough element was in each locality; further, it shows that law officials feared these unsavory forces and apparently went out of their way to avoid them.

> I don't know why, but the area back there was just rougher. They wouldn't take much off of you. I tried to be apart from that culture, but when I went anywhere I was a part of it. I never backed up for nothing. You don't back away from nobody and you don't look off. A person won't hardly shoot you at all if you are looking right in their eyes. A fellow come to town once—a law officer from Hartford. He said, "Those boys on the corner are pretty noisy."

It wasn't me; was some of the others that was with me. But we was on all four corners of the square. He said, "I'd lock them up."

A great big policeman here at Washington said, "Yeah, that's what you think." Said, "I won't put them in jail. You won't hear them saying nothing nasty. And they're drinking some awful good whiskey—100 to 110 proof straight corn whiskey, dry malt."

He said, "Do you drink it?"

And he said, "When I want it, I do. They give it to me."

"Why," he said, "I'd lock them up."

He said, "No you wouldn't either. There's no way. A rabbit could run across that square and they'd kill it a-running. And they've got better guns than you've got." Said, "The best thing you can do if they come up there is to leave them alone." Said, "They don't bother nobody and nobody bothers them. We've got that all worked out."

One time they was trying a murder case at the courthouse, and a bunch of us was summoned as witnesses. Now there was two bunches of them Goinses out there, and they was three of them killed. Tempers were pretty high. They put us in the jury room. They knew we had some guns on us, and they told us to leave them in the sheriff's office. They were going to search everybody that went in the courtroom— Circuit Court. Course we had some whiskey, too. Everybody had a bottle of whiskey in his pocket. So we come up there. Got to the top of the stairs and they's a big bunch waiting to see what we was going to do.

The law said, "You're not going in there without us searching you." Said, "You go back down to the sheriff's office and leave them guns."

I said, "Put us in that room like a bird in a cage and you'll turn the cat in on us." I said, "No way! We don't have nothing in it, but there's nobody going to open that door and start shooting at us and kill a bunch of us. The first time that door opens and somebody starts shooting, we're going to kill them regardless of who it is." I said, "Get back out of the way!" I pushed him back and all of us went right on into the room.

The judge batted his eyes before court started. He said, "What kind of fellows are you?"

I said, "We're pretty good fellows, Judge."

He said, "You're awful noisy in there." Well, while I was talking to him, I slipped him a pint of corn whiskey, 110 proof, in a sack. I said, "Now, Judge, when you get a chance, you sample what's in this sack." I said, "You won't pay any attention to us making that noise." Now that was a circuit judge! That's the reason they never called me tough. I always got along with them.

It wasn't very long until he was batting his eyes and going on [joking]. He come to the door after a while. They'd close the door to our room, and we'd open it to see what was going on. He come to the door and stuck his head in, said, "I don't mind if you just open the door slightly, but you're opening it more than six inches, and all your heads is up and down looking through there." He said, "They're criticizing my court."

We said, "All right, Judge, we'll be nice."

He cleared up his throat just as big as anything. They didn't know that I had give it to him. Well, court adjourned for dinner. Course, now, we didn't have no sides in this. We lived out there with them [the litigants], see, in a small community. We come out, and there was the deputy sheriff. He said, "Well, boys, you made it till noon, but you won't make it this afternoon.

I said, "I wouldn't bet too much on it." (They had spittoons then. This old lawyer could spit from away off and hit it.) He said, "I'll give you to understand, when you bother one of them, you've got your hands full." He said, "That judge will put you in jail as certain as you're standing there now." He had an idea what I'd done for that judge, don't you see. He said, "They ain't no pain about that judge and he's a good man." Said, "You'd better leave them alone." Said, "You'd get killed, anyway." Said, "I'll defend every one of them if you bother them." Said, "What are these boys doing? Why do you need to feel in their pockets? They haven't bothered anybody."

"Well, I guess it's orders from the court."

Said, "Who is the court? They're a part of it, and I am." Said, "Be back here at one o'clock."

Well, we run out of whiskey. And the big old courthouse windows was large. And right down there below was the walk on the back side of the courthouse. I said, "Say, young fellow, tell your dad to come by here." He was about six or seven years old. His dad come by, and I said, "We need three pints."

"Okay."

A fellow come by and throwed a rope up there. We got it. He went on. Along come a girl with a basket and tied the rope to it, and "whish," we had three pints. I had told the judge, "Judge, if you get a little dry, we've got some more." After court adjourned, the judge asked us, "How in the hell did you get that up there in that room?" He was from Summers County—Hartford.

I said, "Why, they throwed a rope up there and put it in a basket and we pulled it up."

He said, "You're smarter than anybody else in here."

Violence was not something just for public exhibition only, as when the hell-raisers were drinking, boasting, carousing, and flashing guns and knives at social functions. Such displays were window dressing for domestic or home-related death scenes, both on the farms and in the logging and sawmilling camps. Information about violent behavior that had been enculturated during childhood was implemented during adulthood when many area residents resorted to killing to ease their anger and frustration. Virtually all of the homicides described on the following pages were very private matters that involved some aspect of family economy or emotional associations surrounding hearth and home.

The absence of a clear-cut system for allocating people and property[1] led to a domestic quarrel over the parceling out of a dead woman's personal belongings in the Bear River Valley. The result was the shooting death of the deceased woman's sister and brother-in-law at the hands of the women's brother. The victims were Lilly (Ball) Billings and Abe Billings, the killer was Eli Ball, and the place was the Balls' childhood home at the head of Sunken Fork Creek, of which Eli claimed ownership at the time. Oral sources indicated that Lilly and Abe had recently moved in with her sister and husband, Wilma and Big Les Washam, on Honey Creek. Prior to that they had lived with Eli, who tired of the arrangement and ordered them to leave the premises, bellowing that "he didn't want them laying around there, stinking." Eli warned them, according to one source, that should they come back, they were "to bring their coffins with them." Eli himself was not remembered in much better terms by at least one narrator, who claimed that he was so foulmouthed and high-tempered that whenever his team of mules would not perform according to his expectations, "he'd run around and bite their ears. He was just foolish that way."

Eli had come into ownership of the Ball homeplace through a procedure questioned by other members of the family. Nell (Ball) Washam died intestate in late 1918 but reportedly wanted her brother Eli to have the family farm, which she had earlier obtained by inheritance. In her final minutes, she had written "From Nell to Eli" across the face of the old deed and handed it to Eli. But Lilly and Abe were not satisfied with that procedure, nor with the way that her parents' personal belongings had been divided. Burning with resentment, the two had gone back to her old homeplace, where Eli lived, to get some pieces of her parents' furniture. That was a fatal mistake.

Two neighbors heard the shots that killed Lilly and Abe and rushed to the scene of the crime. Both narrators described what happened on that fateful February 19, 1919, a date remembered by one person "because of the three 19s". One account goes like this:

Abe Billings lived way back up on Bear River there, and him and Lilly had come there to Eli's one morning and was looking around and picking up things that Nell might have had. And they said that Eli's wife hollered down to him in the field and said, "Now, Eli, you'd better come on here and take care of this deed. They're going to get in the trunk and take it."

Eli come on right up there to the house, they said, a-whistling. Went on in the house and reached up over the door and got the shotgun down and some shells, and walked to the door. And Abe Billings was setting right there in a chair. And he shot Abe in the side. And Lilly was out there somewhere, and she run to Abe. And Eli shot her. He shot the muscle of her arm off and her right breast. And shot a hole in her back. That was in 1919.

And me and another boy was down there at the creek playing, and we heard the shots fired and heard the screams and rushed right on up to the house, you know. And she was laying in there screaming to the top of her voice. Well, little Dr. Stacy of Jessetown got there. He came up through there just a-running his horse full speed. And he examined this arm and breast, and he turned her over to see if there was anything wrong on the other side. And he seen there was a hole there in her back. And he run his finger in there to see what direction the bullet went. I was standing there looking, you know. He seen the way the bullet had gone. She was just a-screaming to the top of her voice then. And Abe was laying out there dead, dead as he could be. The doctor said, "Well," and just began to shake his head. And he just turned her back over and give her a dose of medicine, and she just e-e-e-ased off as easy as could be.

So Eli run off that night. We was all scared that he'd come to our house back there on the mountain. We kept the coal oil lamp blowed out as much as we could, for we was all afraid that he'd come back there.

But he went on and give up at Jessetown. And I heard them try him. He said, "I meant to kill Abe, but I was shooting old black powder shells." And he said, "When I shot Abe I meant to kill him, but the smoke just fogged out there till I couldn't see. And I seen an object there, moving." (See, Lilly run to Abe, you know, went to working with him.) Said, "I seen an object out there, moving, and I just kept a-shooting." And he shot her twice, and boy I mean to tell you, it was awful. Abe was a-laying there on his left side, and the blood had just run out there until it had caked up and just looked like something's liver. I never seen the like in all my life."

Eli served a sentence in the state penitentiary, then returned to the valley for the remainder of his life. A crumbling log foundation remains to this day at his old homeplace as a mute reminder of the double killing that occurred there.

The settings for the killings during the 1920s and 1930s seemed not to matter, as about equal numbers died in agricultural surroundings, at moonshining locations, at logging and sawmilling operations, and at social functions. A local store was the scene of a fatal altercation on December 11, 1925, between Robert Beck and Norman Washam; as in numerous other instances, whiskey was a precipitating factor. The place was Beck's grocery store, located in Sugar Grove between Bell Fort and Mattis. Beck and Washam lived in the same locality and were friends. Narrators felt that the matter of a store debt would never have been broached had the two of them not been out drinking together. As one of them told it:

Beck owned a store over there between Bell Fort and Mattis. So Norman Washam and Robert Beck come up there to Alvin Odle's one time. Scott Beardly took them up there, and they drank whiskey and was partly drunk. And they got a little drunker. Went back down to the store, and Robert Beck and Norman got into it at the store over a little debt that maybe Norman owed there. They would never have named it if it hadn't been for whiskey, you know.

Norman was a knifer. He'd knife you. And he drawed his knife and was cutting Robert awful bad before Robert could get on around behind the counter to his pistol. When Robert got there, he got his pistol and shot Norman dead. Robert himself was bleeding to death. They got him to the house. And, you know, they's a verse in the Bible that stops blood—Ezekiel 6, or something. And he told his wife to get the Bible.

And she said, "Why, Robert, they ain't a Bible on the place!" Said, "I've told you and told you to get one."

"Well," he said, "we never did need one till right now." [Laughter]

Washam bled to death there in the store. Friends of the dead man's family took his body to the home of Melba Nena Beck, near the scene of the crime, to be prepared for burial. Since she was Washam's aunt, Beck and Washam were apparently cousins. An interesting aside has it that Washam's brother Vernon, who was hiding from the law at the time, slipped with gun in hand into the room containing the corpse to bid goodbye to his dead brother.

The scene of another killing near that time was at the head of Hat Hollow in Brake County at the confluence of Hemp and Bran creeks. From all indications, it took place in the early 1920s, maybe as late as 1924. The victim was Leon Billings, who had earlier shot and killed Carl Rothman at Tall Rock during a rival lovers' quarrel over a woman. Billings was the grandson of Bart Billings, and the nephew of Cleo, Eb, and Hazel Billings. He was also a first cousin of Nena Slayton, who was Hazel's daughter. All of these relatives were involved as victims, assailants, or both, in killings that occurred during the first four decades of the twentieth century. The Billingses originated in the Bear River Valley, where "they owned a lot of farm land. But they were tough people—about as tough as they walked."

Oral evidence is fairly strong that Leon Billings was stealing hogs, cattle, and corn from Bull Talbot, Ben Emory, and perhaps others who were grazing livestock on open range on Rutherford Mountain. "Leon was living good but not having to work, and people wouldn't put up with it back then." He was killed from ambush, reportedly by five young men from the upper reaches of Honey Creek and nearby Rutherford Mountain, perhaps in response to the reward money offered by Ben

Emory. Those usually incriminated in the killing are Ben Talbot, Charles Talbot, Ransie Lyons, Horace Bartley, and Bos
Husted. The brother of one of the five was tight-lipped about
the matter, and shared only a paucity of details. He did say,
however, that both Bos Husted and Ben Talbot told him what
happened. A resident of Rocky Valley said of these five men,
"I'll tell you, you couldn't tell who was who when they was
together. All they done was make moonshine liquor and any
kind of meanness they wanted to do. That's all they done for a
living."

The ambush occurred as Billings and his wife were on their
way home to Deer Pen Hollow, a branch of Hat Hollow, in
Kentucky. They had been to the Ben Emory store to have some
corn ground into meal. Each was riding a jenny and balancing
a "turn," or sack, of meal in front of them. Mrs. Billings was
also carrying some onion sets in her hands. The fullest of the
oral accounts surrounding the killing runs as follows:

Leon Billings was stealing Bull Talbot's hogs. That was the tale
back then. And he stole them all but one old sow, and when she had
pigs he went back and killed her too. And these fellows waylaid him
over there. They cut out a spot and hid everything behind the ivy
there. They had cut the top of the ivy and everything off. And they
waylaid him there and shot and killed him. Shot him three times.

He had two jennies. He was riding a jenny and his wife was riding a
jenny. The way she [Leon's wife Glade] told it that night, she was
riding and Leon was ahead of her. And they was a big chestnut oak,
and just as soon as they got out from behind that big oak tree, they
fired. One shot hit him right here in the neck. It went in and hit his
neck bone and divided it, and, boy, it tore a hole out of his neck. Glade
run off.

They was shooting round shells. And then the next one hit him
right here in the chest. I found the shell in there. It traveled from one
side of the chest to the other, but it came around the chestbone. And it
hadn't even tore the shell away, as you could feel the crimp right in
there. I felt it myself. And one shot hit a bush and tore up and splat-
tered him with shot. I picked some of the shot out of him. I brought
them home and put them in a little bottle and set it up on the mantle.
It went on and I didn't know it was taking some kind of effect on me—
that shot up there. I'd catch myself looking out the window [afraid].

And I took them out and scattered them out in the yard, and that was the last of them.

Me and my daddy went to get Carl Parrigan and we all went back there and hunted for Leon. It was one dark night. [The narrator's sister interrupted, "It was in March, for the wind was just a-roaring like a storm."] We had an old oil lantern that wouldn't throw light from here to that chair.

We finally got a sled and went and found him, and we came back. And my daddy got Gar Christie to go on his horse down to Stonybrook and call the sheriff to come and hold an inquest. And the sheriff just said to bring him in [to the jail]. So we went back and got Gar Christie and his horse and sled, and we brought him to his home over there.

One additional oral account provides a keen insight into the apparently calloused manner with which the assassins viewed death:

The Billingses had these little jacks or jennies. Well, at the forks of the branch they stopped to get a drink and, God, these men fired on them. Two of the Talbots shot him. He rolled off dead. His wife wasn't afraid of them. She jumped right to her husband's head when he fell in that water.

The others said to Lyons, "You didn't shoot, did you."

And Lyons shot him after he was done down and her bending over him. They was fixing to kill him because he didn't shoot. He wanted to get in on that money, but they found out that he hadn't shot him.

Now this Ben Talbot would get drunk and tell how that jack would bray, you know, over that fresh blood when he shot Billings.

There is neither oral nor written evidence to indicate that anyone was ever charged in connection with the Billings shooting. Three persons freely shared the fact that neighbors were afraid of Billings, and one testified that they "nearly rejoiced when he was killed." His jenny was caught and taken home by the Talbots, who finally killed it and put bed pillows under its head during some sort of drunken pranking session.

Social conditions in the logging and sawmilling camps were more conducive to violence than was typically the case elsewhere in the State Line country. Because persons in the camps were in constant personal contact under unfamiliar circumstances,[2] knifings, beatings, shootings, and rough behavior in general were common. Deaths resulted in a number of instances. Buffalo Lick Hollow stood out in this regard, although Hat Hollow and the bi-state area along the headwaters of the Little Piney Fork River were almost as notorious. Sometimes the neighbors who lived adjacent to the camps had to be on the alert against the loggers and millworkers. At other times trouble was initiated from within the camps by persons living there. Members of the timber industry's management families were not exempt in this regard, as in the instance of Bunt Groce. Bunt was the unprincipled son of Cap Groce, manager of Caleb Cooperage Company, which produced white oak staves for whiskey barrels; it was located in Brake County at a place near the state line called Lonesome.

The first recorded indication of Bunt's unruly behavior came in 1916, when he was involved in the accidental shooting death of a young woman teacher at a Maurley school function. The school was located in the mountains of southern Brake County, two miles southwest of Mt. Gilead. Among the local residents who lived in the school district was a large family of Hills, described as "good people." The Hill cemetery in Mt. Gilead contains a gravestone bearing the inscription, "Louvenia Hill, December 13, 1893, October 31, 1916." Vennie, as she was called, was mortally wounded that evening in October 1916 at a box supper conducted to raise money for school needs.

The fun of the evening was shattered by some drunks, the likes of whom were generally present at such social functions. Included among the troublemakers were Bunt Groce, Claxton Langness, a couple of Talbot boys from Grandview Rock House, and Vennie's brother Claxton. Claxton Hill and Bunt began fighting during the course of the evening, and when Vennie stepped between them to discourage the trouble, she was hit by the bullet intended for her brother. A woman who was there said that "Vennie bled to death as they carried her home. She prayed all the way until she died. The drunk man that killed her came clear after the trial." Another party emphasized that Bunt's release was due entirely to his father's money and the work of a smart lawyer: "He got him out of that by getting a bunch of people to swear a bunch of stuff that wasn't right."

The Hill family's grief did not end with the tragedy of Vennie's death. Claxton died a few years later at the hands of an assassin, thought by some to have been a Staton from nearby Coonsfork.

Six years after Vennie's death, Bunt Groce was indicted on an unrelated "willful murder" charge in the Brake Circuit Court for the October 10, 1922, slaying of Jes Crawley during another fracas at Maurley school. Bunt was again acquitted of murder in January 1925, after filing an Affidavit for Continuance, in which he stated that Autry Baylanch of Rocky Valley shot Crawley during a fight involving several people, and that certain named witnesses—if they were present to testify—would verify his story and exonerate him. Autry Baylanch had already been indicted but he, too, was acquitted.

Bunt was again indicted for "shooting without wounding, but with intent to kill Bryan Botts and David Hulse" in June 1932. Bunt was arrested, tried by jury, and for a third time found not guilty. In 1936 he was indicted for carrying a concealed weapon. Interestingly enough, he was appointed town marshall of Washington not long afterward.

Events similar to those involving Groce were occurring with regularity across the line in Tennessee. In 1923, Ish Hawthorne killed a fellow named Laine in Buffalo Lick Hollow as they worked near each other for separate logging outfits. Although the motive for the killing was not specified, and no charges were filed against the assailant, it was claimed that Laine was killed with his own gun: "Laine had a gun and Hawthorne wanted to see it. He handed it to Hawthorne, and Hawthorne shot him. Don't know why." A person who was working with Hawthorne at the time recalled a subsequent event in which Hawthorne bluffed Laine's revenge-minded brothers into thinking that he had a gun in his pocket:

After the killing, me and Hawthorne was walking through here by them Talbots on the state line and on down into Buffalo Lick Hollow.

Come to these two fellows setting on the railroad track down there—one on each side. And Ish told me, "You get behind."

And I got behind. He was wearing overalls. He run his hand down in his overalls—had his hand in his britches, sort of bulgy like. And I didn't know what was taking place. We passed them, walked by. I spoke to them. I didn't know them. I'd speak to anybody! When we got by them, he said, "You get in front." We got on down the road, and he laughed a little sniggle and said, "I'll tell you, a little bluff will work sometimes."

I said, "Why?"

He said, "That was Laine's brothers up there and they would have killed me. They wudn't pretending. They both had guns."

He didn't even have a gun!

I was seventeen years old then. That would have been about 1923.

Also in Buffalo Lick Hollow in the 1920s, Bartin Billings—whose involvement in killing a woman and throwing her body in a hole was previously described—was shot and killed from ambush while he was standing on a stack of lumber at Abraham's mill. No one knew who shot him from a ridge overlooking the mill, nor were they willing to speculate regarding the assassin's identity. One person did say, however, that Billings had recently fallen out with Jes Washam. Another narrator commented matter-of-factly, "When they got mad at somebody, they'd just go up on the hill and shoot them and go on about their business."

The first killing instigated in or adjacent to any of the sawmilling camps by the presence of women took place on May 2, 1925,[3] when Joshua "Cap" Brannan killed Boris Beary over Brannan's wife. Not long prior to the shooting, Brannan had built a box cabin on the exact site where Thurgood Talbot's cabin had stood when he was shot from ambush by Eb Nesbitt. Joshua was Carlson Brannan's son by Thurgood Talbot's widow, Sally Nesbitt Talbot Bowles, and Carlson had raised Joshua. One person recalled going to Carlson Brannan's home several years earlier to buy some tobacco and seeing Joshua as a little fellow. "He run back under the bed," he said, "and got back under there and growled and barked and yelled around like a dog at all of us. His black eyes were just a-shining, a-peeping out from under the bed at us."

Boris Beary lived in Abraham's camp; he was married but keeping rather steady company with Brannan's wife, it was claimed. The fateful confrontation took place following a lot of heavy drinking in the camp. One narrator had quit working there just one week prior to the killing because of the excessively heavy drinking and untamed behavior on the weekends. Matters had gotten so bad that "Brannan finally bought him a new pistol. He took all he was going to from the crew down there [at the mill]. On this Saturday they all got drunk and Cap [Brannan] left and went to the house." Beary apparently followed him home and was killed when he attempted to force entry. A man who inspected the scene of the killing picked up the story at that point:

Cap Brannan killed Boris Beary over here in Buffalo Lick Hollow. My dad owned that land in there. And I'd went over there. Dad moved Beary's body. He fell on the steps at the front door, and Joshua jumped out over him and run off down in the hollow. They called the bloodhounds. When I got over there, Beary was laying there on the steps. I seen a knife laying there by him, I said, "Whose knife is that?"

Someone said, "It's his'n; it's Beary's knife."

Carter Cross picked it up and throwed it in the wagon. And I stepped into the house after they got him up and loaded him into the wagon to haul him out. I said, "By God, here's his cap behind the door. He was in the house!"

They said, "Yes, he was in the house and he turned around to the door when Brannan shot him and put his hands up on the door and fell backwards on the steps."

Joshua had that to do [i.e., kill Beary]. At least he thought he did. Beary was drunk, and he'd went up there to Joshua's house. And he started in there on Joshua, and there wasn't but one door to the house. And Joshua couldn't get out, so he shot him. Wudn't but one door to the house.

And Joshua's wife waited to get out, and they had to take a plank off of the back side of the house. It was just a logging camp house—thin walls. She didn't want to step over the body because he was dead. She was ready to have a baby in just about a month.

Brannan was sentenced to the state penitentiary for life but was paroled early. His wife divorced him soon after the killing and later remarried. She died in 1970. Joshua, too, married again and lived to be an old man, dying in the mid-1970s. Beary's widow also remarried at her husband's death and lived to be more than 90 years old.

Allegedly, there were other killings in the 1920s, generally in the sawmilling camps, but most of these will not be described here because of insufficient documentation. The date and cause of Ben Christie's death, for example, are uncertain. His body was reportedly found just south of the state line at the head of Honey Creek sometime in the 1920s. Christie boasted that he could drink a quart of whiskey, the story goes, and some fellow countered with the offer, "If you'll drink it, I'll buy it for you." Christie proceeded to drink it, then went off over the hill and died: "He just fell off the horse and died there, drunk. They wudn't any marks on him." But another narrator disagreed with the last statement. "I knowed him and knowed his wife," she stated. "Me and my sister went up there that evening as he lay a corpse. They never did find out who killed him. Just found him dead. Said he had been beat with clubs." No arrests were made.

In the mid-1920s, one reported event of rape and another of niece-beating or possible rape led to the separate shooting deaths of Jes and Autry Baylanch, unmarried brothers who grew up in Brake County just across the mountain from Rocky Valley. Both were likely about 30 when they were killed: the federal census lists Autry as born in 1894 and Jes in 1897. It is thought that Jes died as a penalty for raping Nuland Merton's wife, a beautiful young woman who had grown up in Waterfall. "She had the prettiest blond hair I ever saw on anybody's head," stated a narrator who had known her since childhood. Mrs. Merton had been visiting her parents in Waterfall and, with one or two of her children, began walking to her home located in a little oilfield in Washam Hollow, some two miles to the east. All of the narrators believed that she had been attacked by two persons, but they were not in agreement as to the identities of the two. Some said that they were the Baylanch brothers, Jes and Autry. Others claimed they were Jes Baylanch and Bos Husted. Whoever the guilty ones were, "they took her off the road and mistreated [raped] her, and somebody passed by and heard the child a-crying." Indications are that only Jes Baylanch abused her sexually before she managed to escape. She reportedly stated later that she "heard them coming for her again, and she run and hid in a tree top. They thought she'd hid. Said they even set fire to the tree top to see if they could locate her. But she got away and got back to her home."

Her enraged husband, who himself had been indicted in the Brake Circuit Court in 1916 for carrying a concealed deadly weapon, maintained a death vigil that night. Why he expected Baylanch to come to the Merton home (or why Jes would want to come) was not made clear by the narrators; perhaps Merton feared that Baylanch might try to get to his wife again. In any case Mrs. Merton's brother was there to assist her husband with the job that he vowed would be done. "Said they set there, right still. Said Merton was expecting Jes to come. Jes was rough. Said they had the door pulled just about a third open. Directly, they heard Jes walk up on the porch. And just as he stepped around the dark of the door, Merton shot him down right on the porch."

One narrator observed that Merton and his brother-in-law left the scene of the killing that night without reporting their crime to anyone, and Baylanch's body was not discovered for two or three days. It was said that the case never came to trial, and no record of an indictment is to be found in the Brake County court records. In a culture that had its own code of retributive folk justice, Baylanch's bad reputation was enough to keep the case out of court.

The nature of Autry Baylanch's violation against his niece, Cora Washam, was not known to the narrators. Opinions were divided in the matter. Some said that Autry whipped her; others stated simply that he "mistreated" her. It may be that he raped her or at least attempted to. One person perhaps intimated as much when he described Cora as "an awful pretty little girl," and another stated that "she wasn't married." Whatever the nature of the act, she "went home and told Vernon [her father] about it."

The Washam home was in or near a Tennessee Stave and

Lumber Company logging camp on Little Nick Creek in the eastern part of the Bear River Valley. Baylanch lived there, too, in a boardinghouse operated by Penrod Baylanch, relationship unknown. "Old Man Penrod Baylanch said they was setting there one morning. Said Autry had been on a drunk the day before. Hadn't even worked. Autry was rough. And Penrod had just got breakfast ready and they was all setting around the little old table they had."

"And Autry didn't want no breakfast," another added. "He was a-setting there sorta out in the front room. And Old Vernon, Autry's uncle, jumped to the front door, him and his boy, and said to Autry, 'I said if you ever bothered my family, I'd kill you, and I'm a-going to,' then shot him through and through. I saw where the bullet went. It went through two pieces of oak lumber."

Another narrator, seemingly in defense of Baylanch, claimed that when Washam walked to the kitchen door, Baylanch's back was turned to him: "He was eating and Washam shot him. He just walked to that door and shot Autry with that shotgun. And Autry had set and watched him load that shell [replace the shot with a slug]. He loaded it to keep the law away from where they was making whiskey, and Autry said, 'Don't shoot me no more. You've done killed me.' And Washam told him, 'That's what I come here for.' And he just left."

Washam went to Bell Fort and had someone there call the sheriff of Fountain County. It was claimed that the sheriff reassured him and instructed him to "go back and kill some more of them [Baylanches]. We don't want them here." The same attitude of indifference and disgust had been expressed by the Brake County deputy, who asked that the body of Leon Billings be brought to him to save him the trouble of going to the scene of the crime.

Both Autry and Jes Baylanch were buried adjacent to the Tunk Cemetery near Waterfall, but outside the enclosure fence. Community sentiment against them would not permit their interment within the formal bounds of the cemetery. (When the burial ground was expanded in recent years, however, the fence was then extended to enclose their graves. Their burial sites were never marked with stones, but vital statistics records indicate that Autry was killed June 24, 1925.[4]

Jes and Autry Baylanch were members of a very large, extended family that lived on both sides of the state line near Rutherford Mountain. The numerous indictments against the Baylanches in the 1920s and 1930s attest that their behavior was seldom acceptable to those who lived around them. These "half Indians," as they were described, carried guns and knives and wielded them freely. Claims that the Baylanches were both killers and victims on several occasions can likely be attributed to the fact that they trafficked heavily in moonshine whiskey as makers, sellers, and consumers. Like the Talbot, Bowles, Pannings, and Husted families, among others on Rutherford Mountain, the Baylanches were more prone to hunt than farm, to make whiskey than stalk game. They guarded their little whiskey kingdom against all encroachers and reportedly shot to kill when strangers got too close.

The Baylanches were not above "using" local law enforcement officials through trickery and deception, even if it meant the death of a neighbor and friend who represented competition to their illegal whiskey enterprise. Gee Baylanch, clan patriarch, was accused of reporting Bing Tarter, a 51-year-old whiskey-making neighbor, to the law and then assisting as a special deputy while Tarter was—according to public opinion—inexcusably gunned down by deputy Cleo Parks. That event took place more than 50 years ago, on January 24, 1933. Yet the people of the area have neither forgotten nor forgiven Parks and Baylanch for their unacceptable manner of handling the situation. Four oral texts provide not only graphic detail but also attitudes toward deceit, betrayal, the inherent right to make whiskey, and interference by the law. The first three statements were provided by lifelong residents of the area; the fourth came from a former county judge.

I've heard a whole lot about these killings. Them people that made whiskey would get jealous of each other and kill one another, too, over the selling of it. Maybe one made it a little better than the other'n, and he'd get the most trade. And they might take the notion to just get rid of him.

Back then, there was a little boy. Now I don't know whether this happened or not. Said the lawmen, "Boy, where is your dad?" He told them where he was at, back up there on the hill. And they told him that they'd give him 50 cents if he'd tell them. And he told them he would.

They hadn't give it to him yet. He said, "You ain't give me my 50 cents yet." Wouldn't tell them.

They said, "Well, we'll pay you as we come back."

"No, no, no," he said. "All that goes up there don't come back." He wanted that money before he went.

Gee Baylanch caused a lot of trouble. He was the cause of Cleo Parks killing Bing Tarter. They said that Tarter admitted that he had been making moonshine, and said, "Come on down here and I'll show you what I've been doing." Said, "I've got a still right down here."

Well, Bing picked his gun up, and his wife hollered and told the law, "There ain't no shells in it. He's drunk." But they went ahead and shot him. Gee was afraid of him.

There was a fellow at Waterfall by the name of Bing Tarter. And Bing was one of the politest fellows you'll ever see. But all he done was make whiskey.

Had a deputy sheriff at Lightsboro name of Cleo Parks. Cleo come up through the Waterfall community that day. And Dale Turney and Tom North and Gee Baylanch didn't like Bing. So Cleo come along and told them, "I've got a warrant for Bing Tarter. I've got to go up there and arrest him."

He took the three with him. It didn't suit Bing much, as he didn't want to be arrested by his enemies. He just opened fire on them and they had to kill Bing. The deputy sheriff killed Bing.

Bing Tarter was a brave man, and was involved some in bootleg-ging in the Coonsfork area—Waterfall side. Parks was deputy sheriff. Went up there and I reckon took no chances. Just killed him. Parks was pretty trigger happy, to tell the truth about it. So whether he gave Tarter a chance or not, I don't know.

The last narrator's wife added that a former sheriff's wife had told her that her sheriff-husband had arrested Tarter many times, and added that "he was just as meek as a mouse."

These statements by persons who knew Tarter assume additional meaning when weighed against the fact that Bing Tarter himself was a frequent violator of law and order. At least four warrants for his arrest were issued between 1927 and 1933: one for living in adultery; one for interfering with the election process at Waterfall "by drawing guns and pistols and shooting in and around the voting house"; a third for shooting at another resident in the locality with intent to kill; and a fourth for "maliciously shooting at" another person with intent to kill. In the last instance, the case against Tarter was dropped, as he had already been sentenced to a term in the penitentiary on still another violation. Despite these charges against Tarter, the fact that he was betrayed by a neighbor and gunned down by the law made him guiltless in the eyes of the local people. They still feel that way.

Any mention of Gee Baylanch still evokes considerable talk among the people of the State Line country. Few persons here are more talked about than this notorious character. Gee, born in 1872, was married to Nanny Washam, who bore him four children. He also had an illegitimate child, a son called Foxey. At Foxey's birth, Gee took him to Nanny and reportedly told her that he was to be raised right along with the other children.

It was said that Gee's boys were into all sorts of trouble both while they were growing up and in later life. Killings were attributed to Gee and the boys in far greater abundance than could be documented, as court charges were apparently not always brought against them. It may be that people attributed violence to them because of their reputation. Court records are filled, in fact, with entries regarding their misbehavior in public and their moonshining activities. Whether or not they actually killed people as claimed is really inconsequential to the legend, since the narrators believed it. On the basis of rumor, one person reported of the Baylanches, "I've heard it said that back there on the mountain, if they found somebody riding a pretty nice horse, they'd just dump his body over that cliff and take his horse." That statement was corroborated by a neighbor of the Baylanches, who passed along rumor and then claimed that he personally saw the body of a man whom Gee and his boys had killed:

On back there astraddle the state line in the wilderness, a stranger come along and was staying up there baching in a logging camp cabin. You could stay in them, or just drop over the side of a cliff and stay in one of the rock houses. But he was staying there. The Baylanches was wondering about him. Well, they borrowed a man's .30-.30 rifle one day, took the shells and took the hull or bullet out of one of them. They shot him in the back. When he fell, they got some money off of him, then took him down there and buried him. That got them [Gee and boys] started.

Everytime they'd find a stranger along there, they'd kill him. Once, they took all of the clothes off of this man but his underwear. If they had gold in their mouth, they'd knock that out. And sometimes they didn't bother about burying them. They just took them to the side of the road and throwed them over—throwed them out on the breeze.

This was in the late 1920s. They was mean. I never thought too much about them, I reckon. I lived around out there, and I figured I was as mean as they was. They lived way on out there from us. I was coming along one day, and they was about four of them. They was awful noisy when they was drinking. One of them says to me, "Come out here, I want to show you something."

I had to ride in front of them! I didn't want to, for I wanted to be among them. I figured if they didn't shoot me through the head, I'd kill two or three of them before I fell. I'm not bragging, but I was the best shot in that country.

They turned off and went out on a point 300 or 400 feet from the road. I was riding a mean mule and it just started rearing up and standing up on its hind feet. One of them said, "Look there." About 20 feet ahead they was a man laying there, and the maggots were so bad that it looked like he was breathing. That was the awfulest odor you ever smelled. They said, "Now, that's what a man gets for coming through here."

They wudn't going to bother me, I don't reckon, but I tried to watch them. When we turned to leave, that mule of mine wouldn't stay in the crowd. It had to get in front of them! When we got out a little ways, they went out one way, and I come on out by Grandview Rockhouse.

I don't know how many they did kill out there. The law never handled them for this. They got pretty close to two of them on the last one, though. They never did kill no more.

Another time, a fellow by the name of Babe Vertrees was courting

Gee's oldest daughter. They always come out from where they lived by way of Waterfall post office. That was a busy place in those days, and just about as tough as they ever was. They was seven or eight killed every year there around that neighborhood.

He rode up on his horse and got off and said, "I want you to look at one thing. When Gee Baylanch comes down here, he's got a pinstriped suit on. You look right in the middle of his back and you'll find a patch." He said, "That was my rifle that killed that man." Said, "Shot him in the back." He said, "Now, he'll have a patch on it."

And Gee's just about as tough a man as ever walked. He come on down there, just a-blowing [bragging] and a-talking, you know. That was the first day of court, and they all used to come in then. And this person [at the store] would say something to get Gee to turn around, and this one would say something over here. And everybody got him to turn around. He got off his horse, and there the patch was! I was on the porch within about three feet of him. Some of them men just a-looking, and there it was, just a little patch. Pretty pinstriped suit.

Frank Baylanch, somehow related to all the others of that name in the State Line country, lived on Skillet Creek just across the mountain from Brownsville. He was married to Susie Washam. Their son Oren, who was born in 1904, was looked upon by others of the area as a very respectable young man, but like most of the other fellows, he liked whiskey. Oren found whiskey and "bad women" in abundance at the "happy home," the local designation for the home of Hascal and Trish (Nesbitt) Pannings, located in Hemp Hollow at Abraham's sawmilling camp. Virtually all of the narrators commented on the loose morals of two of the Pannings girls, and two persons claimed that Trish herself was entertaining male visitors. Of the Pannings home, one narrator stated, "Now, I'm going to tell you, it was just a mess of a place. Pretty rough people." Another commented, "Hascal had two girls that was pretty rough, and men would go there to see them." A third person, speaking from firsthand knowledge, recalled, "Men just gathered in there like a bunch of dogs."

On Saturday night, October 4, 1930, three fellows from the Brownsville area and three from Rutherford Mountain went separately to the "happy home" for an evening of drinking and

Honey Creek-Rutherford Mountain residents, c. 1928. The fellow second from left died in 1930 in a double killing at a house of prostitution on the state line at the head of Hemp Hollow. The man on the left witnessed the event.

sex. Once there, they disagreed over the question of which ones were to be the recipients of the women's affections for the evening. The brawl that followed led to a double killing. Oren Baylanch shot and killed Ben Talbot and was then shot to death by Ben's brother, Lug.

Ben died during the initial burst of gunfire. Oren, who was hit but apparently not mortally wounded, managed to crawl from the house and get a few yards down the road. Everyone in the Pannings house knew immediately of Ben's death, but most assumed that Oren had simply run off to avoid further gunplay. Ben's brother Lug had watched Oren leave, however, and followed the injured man outside. Lug shot Oren and left him for dead in a ditch, but told no one what he had done. A neighbor and close friend of all the fellows present that evening went to the scene of Ben's homicide the next morning to find out what had happened, not knowing that Oren had been shot. He recounted how he and a companion discovered Oren's body, and commented on the fact that people then and now believed that it was not Oren who had killed Ben Talbot:

Lug told me that he helped kill Oren. He shot him. He said that Ben was shot twice. Baylanch was the one that got Ben killed, but his pistol just had one empty shell in it. And Lug said that Ben was shot twice. That's why somebody else shot him once. Said, "I shot Baylanch in the side as I ran around the corner of the house. But I shot him in the side." He was telling me that after the shooting. He said that he run out of [bullets], or pistol hung, or something, "and I couldn't shoot him no more, but I shot him in the side."

And he was shot in the side all right. And they was a bullet in the corner of the house there where Lug said there was. He'd [Baylanch] hit the corner of the house as he went around it. And he said that Baylanch [supposedly] shot twice, but he just had one empty shell in his gun.

Lug said that somebody else shot Ben. He never said who he thought it was. [There was a strong feeling expressed by some of the informants that Hascal Pannings killed Talbot.]

Well, I was over there the next morning, and they didn't know where Oren was. They didn't know whether he's dead or not. And Hascal Pannings told me and Craig Prather over there, said, "He went right up that way. Run off up the hill there in a log-cart road."

Craig said to me, "Let's walk up that-a-way. And we went up that-a-way and found him. He was a-laying in the rut there where they had been snaking logs. He was laying there. And he had pulled his coat off and put it under his head. When we found him, he was dead.

Both Oren and Ben were buried in the Baylanch Cemetery on the same day and at the same hour. During the course of the service, Ben Talbot's mother came by to view Oren's corpse. She was heard to say, with sadness in her voice, "I'm a Baylanch, too," thus indicating that her son had killed a relative. It was revealing to learn that "Oren's folks wouldn't go by to look at Ben's body"; they felt superior to the Talbots. A Reverend Black conducted Baylanch's funeral, but no minister was there to preside at Talbot's graveside rites. His casket did not go unattended, however. A person who was present at the double funeral provided a touching account of the manner in which an unlettered mountain preacher from the Bear River Valley stepped into the void to avert embarrassment for Talbot family mourners: "Roscoe Bede was there, and whenever they started carrying them to the graves, they all went in opposite directions. Ben was taken this-a-way and Oren that-a-way. Most of the crowd turned after Oren, and Roscoe started, too, you know. He was a minister. But he saw what was a-happening, so he turned around then and went to Ben's grave to say the prayers. I always felt so good about that."

Ben Talbot had never married, but he was the father of a little boy who was brought to the funeral by the child's mother. When the people present passed by the open casket to view Ben's remains for the last time, the mother held the little boy up and said tearfully, "Look, there's Daddy."

Lug Talbot "scouted" for a while after he killed Baylanch, but he was eventually arrested by lawmen from Owenton County and then turned over to Brake County officials to be charged and tried for the crime. Several informants, feeling that the matter should never have entered the courts, blamed Lug Talbot's conviction for killing Oren on the lawyer assigned to defend him. It was not until Lug confessed that people really believed he was guilty. He was convicted of voluntary manslaughter and sentenced to the Kentucky state penitentiary for 15 years. He later told a narrator of the rough treatment and periods of intense depression that he experienced in prison. "I'll never go back again," he said. "I'd rather be hung up to that tree right there, or tied to it and let them build a big fire and burn me to death, before I go back to the penitentiary." Following his release, Lug moved to Owenton County, where he was still living at the time he committed suicide: "He said when he got to where he couldn't keep his family up, he'd just kill himself. He did, by hanging himself."

A few months previous to the Talbot-Baylanch trouble, a logging camp incident near Waterfall caused the death of Hebron Prather under questionable and unexplained circumstances. He was working at the time as a mule skinner in a mountaintop logging camp in the Blue Hollow section of southern Brake County. About four o'clock on the morning of

January 13, 1928, Prather went to feed his mules but never returned for breakfast. Fellow loggers found him lying on the ground, dead from a bullet wound in the head. Opinion was divided as to the cause of death. Some thought he had slipped and fallen, causing his gun to discharge. Others argued strongly that he had been killed by one of the black men who worked with him, although they could offer no reasons for the man's action. At length, the death was declared accidental. Prather's body was carried off the mountain by other members of the crew and placed in a wagon for the four-mile trip to his home in Pannings Hollow, near Lightsboro.

Six months later, on June 28, 1928, Elmore Christie (closely related to the Christies of Honey Creek) was indicted in the Brake County Circuit Court on a "willful murder" charge for the pistol killing of Ben Goins on Bingham Branch. Several warrants were issued over a period of three to four years for Christie's arrest, but none of them was ever served. Like so many violators during those years, Christie had left the state. A note scribbled across an unserved warrant in 1932 bore the simple message, "In Ohio." One narrator said of Christie in a sympathetic tone, "He was a pretty good fellow. His brother stayed at our house most of the time. They was two pretty good boys, but just had to stay here and yonder." Not only had the speaker excused the presumed killer in his own mind; he also expressed the widespread notion that homeless persons were more likely to go bad.

A domestic killing in the upper portion of the Little Piney Fork River country took place on July 1, 1930, when Sherm "Bud" North was found beaten to death. His brother-in-law, Rod Tarter, was indicted for the homicide but was cleared of the charge in November, when a "not guilty" verdict was rendered by the jury. One narrator insisted that Tarter was guilty, however, and told how he had hit the victim squarely between the eyes "with a sheep skull rock that pushed his whole skull in." The informant claimed that North had kicked Tarter's dog Queenie, and that Tarter, who "could kill squirrels with rocks," warned North that he would kill him in similar fashion if

North ever kicked the dog again. North was unwilling to resist a dare, and Tarter had no intentions of backing down on his threat.

Alcohol consumption was the known cause of a violent death at Brownsville school on the evening of February 7, 1931. The victim that night was Pitt Bede (born 1904), the only son of Mart and Vernie (Christie) Bede and a member of the large Bede clan whose earlier exploits were described in Chapter 1. His killer was Elmo Slayton, a heavy-drinking epileptic who spent much time at his home—located slightly south of the state line near Boyer Mountain—just sitting and brooding. Elmo was the illegitimate son of Rosie Slayton, an unmarried woman in her 40s who divided her time between caring for her son and living with Len Talbot, a local moonshiner.

Slayton killed Bede while religious services were in progress at the Brownsville school. When Pitt Bede attempted to break up a drunken brawl between Slayton and a Lyons fellow, "Elmo just hauled out his pistol and shot Pitt down," according to a witness, who added, "they hadn't said no words."

Slayton was sentenced to the penitentiary by a Trundle County jury, but he died shortly after beginning his term. One narrator had heard that "Elmo wouldn't do what they wanted him to do. So they turned water in on him to make him bail it out or drown. He took pneumonia and died." A second person was more specific: "I heard they put him in a barrel of water," he said, "and put his feet down in there and turned the water on in the barrel. Then they give him cups to dip out the water with, so he could keep it from getting over his face and nose— to keep him from drowning. He took pneumonia and died from that." I have since heard a similar explanation for two additional unrelated prison deaths and thus suspect that the water-bailing story is a migratory legend employed by local folk to comment on Slayton's unexplained death in prison. By this means they can vicariously criticize the legal system that overrode their own code of justice.

Elmo's mother, Rosie Slayton, died violently six years later (in 1937) at the hands of Julie Talbot, Len Talbot's jealous wife. Rosie, born in 1884 to Carl and Hazel (Billings) Slayton, was closely related to Cleo and Bart Billings, whose involvements in violence have already been noted. Additionally, she was the sister of Roy Slayton, who killed Cleo Billings. She was never married, and it was said that she had given her affections rather freely to several men of the area until she took up with Len Talbot, a man to whom she emotionally and physically dedicated herslf for the rest of her life: "They dated for years and years." The fact that she was Len's senior by about 20 years seemed not to matter to either of them.

Len was a brother of Ben and Lug Talbot, the two who were involved in the double-death Talbot-Baylanch shoot-out at the Pannings home. A "short, stocky young man," born about 1905, Len eventually married Julie Rowan, "a little skinny, weakly-looking woman" about his age from Owenton County. They lived in one of the shacks that had been deserted when O.R. Abraham pulled his sawmilling operation out of Hemp Hollow. His marriage notwithstanding, Len continued to see Rosie and lived alternately with the two women, who were extremely jealous of each other; each constantly made disparaging comments about the other. Their conflict was resolved deep within the confines of Rutherford Mountain on May 26, 1937.

Len was "back on the mountain near Overview Rock" making moonshine whiskey with Bos Husted. Rosie Slayton was keeping them supplied with sugar from the Ben Emory store by hauling it to them on the back of a mare. A husband and wife narrator team talked about what happened that day in 1937, both before and after the killing. "Rosie was an awful good person to me," the woman recalled. "She had her mailbox here in front of our house. And the morning she got killed, she stopped to get the mail. She went on up the road with her sack of meal on an old horse." The man, who went to the scene of the killing that took place later in the day, continued at some length:

Rosie come back down by here and went on up here and got some sugar—sack of sugar from Uncle Ben Emory's store—to take back there and make liquor. She was taking it back there to Len. And Bos said him and Len was up there on the mountain waiting for her. The two met her with the sugar. They started on over into Kentucky, but got up there a little piece and were sitting on a log talking, resting. And Bos said that they didn't have no matches for a smoke. Len's daddy lived around the hill, and Len told Bos to go on around there and get some matches.

Bos went, and Len's wife, Julie, was there. Julie told Bos, "Well, I'll go with you."

Said he told her, "Now, Len and Rosie is out here waiting for me, and you'd better not go."

She said, "Yes, I'm going home." And she got the children, two little girls, and started on with Bos. They went on out there and got with the others.

All of them went on together till they got across the state line. Len was riding Rosie's old horse and packing the children. Len stopped when they got into Kentucky, turned and told some of them to take the children down, that he wanted to rest. He was drunk and wanted to rest. They helped the children down. Then Len got down himself. Rosie, she was there. She come over to Len. He was setting there by the side of the road. She got a .22 cartridge from him. She had a .22 gun—packing Len's .22 gun. She got some cartridges out of Len's pockets when Len was setting there. Julie was setting over on the other side of the road. And Rosie throwed the gun up in her face and said, "I'm going to kill you."

Well, Julie just set her baby down and run right under Rosie and stabbed her right in the throat artery with a pocketknife. She was gone in a second.

Another narrator had personally talked with Bos about what happened that day and recalled Bos saying that "Rosie throwed her hands up and screamed, and Bos run and grabbed her, but she was dead by the time he got her to the ground. He said that blood was a-going way up there in the trees." The incident seemingly had little impact on Julie; she calmly picked up her baby, set it on her hip, and walked back to her father-in-law's place. She went inside, sat down, fed her baby some milk and bread as she told him what had happened.

Word of the tragedy spread throughout the immediate area, and neighbors went to the scene both out of curiosity and to help remove Rosie's body from the remote spot. Four-man teams carried her on a folding cot to the Baylanch tavern at the state line, and a waiting vehicle hauled her body down the treacherous road to her home on Bedes Branch, where she was living alone at the time. "She was killed on a Saturday but hadn't been prepared for burial by Sunday. Nora Lyons told me that Rosie's cousin, Wilma Washam, asked her to change Rosie's clothes, wash and prepare the body for burial. Nora told Wilma she would if Nora's mother-in-law would help her. So the two started the job, but finally had to ask Nora's husband Garland to help them. Nora said she got so sick she like to of died. Rosie had laid in her bloody clothes from Saturday until some time Sunday."

One of the narrators who went to the scene of the homicide recalled feeling at the time that the "wrong woman" had been killed: "I told Bos, 'By God, it went the wrong way. You had it made up for Rosie to kill Julie!'" Bos countered, "No, we never even thought about that." Another narrator thought that it was Rosie who had been slated for death all along: "Rumor had it that Len was through with Rosie," she said, "and maybe afraid of her, too."

Attitudes toward Rosie's death were mixed at the time. One informant recalled that she personally was beside herself with joy upon hearing from her husband that Rosie was dead, and loudly exclaimed, "Good, good, good!" Another was saddened, however, and still remembers Rosie with fondness. "She helped me with my children when they were little," she stated, "and if I was washing, she'd jump right in and do my washing and hang it out to dry." A schoolmate of Rosie's took a more moderate position toward the Slayton family in general: "I went to school with Rosie. Now if they liked you, they was good people. If they didn't like you, you'd better not have anything to do with them."

No formal charges were brought against Julie for killing Rosie. She and Len soon moved to Ewell Mountain in Owenton County, where a baby girl was born to them in March 1938. Julie died a few years later from nosebleed—the same affliction that had earlier taken the life of her baby. Len continued to live there following her death, although he later remarried. A

former deputy sheriff of that county told of the time that he
and the sheriff arrested Len for moonshining on Ewell Mountain, in what was Len's last attempt to make whiskey:

> He never done nothing after that. He had this little 12-year-old boy
> with him. Like to scared that little boy to death. Took him to Bowling
> Green [to court], too. The judge popped it to both of them. The boy
> was ordered to go to school. The county judge took him over. The
> woman [welfare agent] that looks after a kid that way wanted me to
> take him. I said, "I can't handle him, I'm an officer."
>
> She said, "You just have him here every first Monday each month
> and I'll talk to him."
>
> They was poor folks and didn't have no clothes fit to wear to school.
> And I went to the store and bought them myself—shoes, shirt, and a
> pair of pants—to go to school. And the little fellow went every day.
> He'd went before, but the other kids would laugh at him because he
> had holes in his clothes.
>
> And they was a little brother. He come the next day to me and said,
> "Would you buy me some pants and shirt and shoes like Sammy?" His
> name was Sammy.
>
> I said, "Yeah," and walked over and bought him some stuff for them
> to eat. There wasn't a bite in the house for them to eat."

At the time of his own death, Len lived alone and had been
working at a beer joint on the state line. His lonely death was
chronicled in a former neighbor's daily log of happenings with
these words, "Len Talbot died in his sleep June 3, 1968. He was
living in a trailer on the Tall Rock Mountain."

Distinctions along class lines were seldom manifested in the
State Line country, not even in the minds of those few persons
who achieved a degree of financial success in farming, logging,
or merchandising. Culturally, these achievers continued to
remain a part of the local mainstream. Since their society
condoned lethal violence, they, too, resorted to the gun in
settling interpersonal/interfamily disputes. In no instance is
this better demonstrated than in the 1931 shooting altercation
in Waterfall, among members of two relatively well-to-do
Goins families, that resulted in two deaths.

The origin of the Goins violence lay in the immediate

post–Civil War era. Mrs. Loretta Alford was left widowed with two sons to care for, the story goes, when her soldier husband was killed in action during the Civil War. She soon married a Goins who was 20 years younger and whom she had "nursed" as a baby. They had two sons, including Eb, who was born in 1869. It was reported that her new husband beat her on repeated occasions—so much, in fact, that a son by her first marriage killed Goins in the late 1880s to end his mother's mental and physical anguish. It was said that Loretta attended her husband's funeral with a badly bruised face.

Eb Goins became a farmer-merchant in Waterfall and—assisted by insurance received at the death of his son during World War I—the "most progressive, prosperous" person in the area. Another of his sons, Blount (born in 1904), was unique in local circles in that he had an automobile. Furthermore, it had a rumble seat! Without question, "he was king of the roost around there." Eb had a first cousin, Blaine Goins, who lived within gunshot range of Eb's store. Blaine, a prominent moonshiner in the community, had a half-dozen children and some grandchildren old enough to dream of riding in Blount's roadster. "So one Sunday morning, Blount come down to some of Blaine's outfit and picked up three or four of Blaine's grandchildren in his car and took them to Tennessee. When he was taking them back home, he got up here to the county line and had a wreck and killed two of them. And that created a bitterness in the family there. . . . Well, late one afternoon [July 13, 1931], Blount and Eb closed the store and started up the road home. Lived up the road about a mile from the store. And Blaine and his boys come out, and they opened fire on them and killed them both."

The father and son were mortally wounded, and both suffered intensely before dying at home. Blount succumbed three days later, Eb on the seventh day. A person who was with them both during their last hours provided a gripping account:

Blount was shot with a shotgun. Cut his arm off, all but some skin, and all the wadding went into his body through his ribs. And when he

Legendary Little Doc Prather lived in Kentucky three miles from Tall Rock. He attended to the needs of numerous victims of shoot-outs and knifings.

breathed, he breathed in and out of that hole. They shot him on Sunday night, and Wednesday morning there wasn't none of us there but two or three boys. And you never heard such hollering, about daylight, in all your life that that fellow was doing. He couldn't speak.

Well, this little Doc Prather, he was an awful good friend of mine. I said [to the other fellows], "I'll tell you what let's do." We didn't fool with bottles of whiskey; we had a half-gallon jar there to keep us going. I said, "Slip in there and get Doc's pouch. We'll give him some morphine just to put him off [let him die]. He can't live."

Well, we slipped in there by the bed and got Doctor's little pouch. I said, "Wash your hands now." Then we poured some whiskey on [the needle]. We kept looking for the morphine. Doc Prather raised up on the bed on his elbow and said, "Is this what you're looking for?" He was too smart for us. He'd had that in his pocket.

He got up and washed his face. We all went outside. Doc couldn't hardly drink whiskey at all without getting drunk. He said, "I'll tell you what I'm going to do. I'm going to take one swallow. Now, don't let me have no more until I'm ready to go." Then he said, "What was you boys going to do?"

I said, "We's figuring on using this distilled water. But if we could have found the pills, we'd have just used this spring water out of the bucket here, and give him two pills to get him out of his misery. He'll never speak. It's awful how that man's suffering." He could hear him hollering. And every time he'd holler, this wadding would come out of his side.

Doc picked up the morphine. He said, "I believe you had a pretty good formula." He dropped two of them in there, shook them a little while till they dissolved. And you know, Blount's voice went down just like something in water sinking. It commenced going down in two minutes, and finally it all disappeared. He went off just as e-e-easy.

And there laid Eb on the porch around from him. Some of them told him about Blount. He didn't have to be watched quite as close. He said, "I know he passed away, I heard him." Eb was shot all to pieces here in the abdomen. He lived several days. Wouldn't go to the hospital, wouldn't do nothing. Nobody wouldn't set up with him. I guess I was too good. I stayed there with him, and he was just about dead. I'd sometimes lay down on the bed with him and go to sleep. And he'd punch me and wake me up. I'd lay my head down on the bed he was in. I thought somebody else could have come in, but they wouldn't do it. He wasn't making no noise. He had too much nerve for that. Ah, he was nervy. He just quit breathing.

They said, "How is he?"

I said, "He's all right, he just quit breathing."

One man come up and looked at him [questioningly] and said, "If he's not breathing, he's dead, isn't he?"

I said, "He's all right now. He's not a-breathing. He quit about 20 minutes ago."

Two of Blaine's sons were indicted twice. The first time was for the shooting death of Blount Goins. After hearing testimony, or lack of it, from 11 persons, the jury rendered a "not guilty" verdict in November 1931. That same day, the two were again indicted, this time for the willful murder of Eb Goins.

That trial, during the March term of the Circuit Court, was to include testimony from 25 persons. Most of them did not show up. A predictable "not guilty" verdict came from the jury.

Tragedy again struck the Goins family on June 30, 1932, when Bert Goins, another of Eb's sons, was shot to death by his brother-in-law, Ernie Boyer. The latter, who later became a very wealthy landowner, had grown to manhood in the small agricultural valley that lay above Rocky Valley. For reasons unstated, Boyer did not like Bert Goins and matters only grew more tense when his sister married Goins. Some of the narrators believed that Goins had mistreated Boyer in various ways, including shooting at him as he went up and down the road in his Chevrolet roadster. Others thought that a boundary dispute between their families was somehow involved. Whatever the problem, Boyer settled it in the manner that had become acceptable in the culture across the years: he shot and killed Goins. The site was the Rocky Valley Methodist Church at a time when church was in session. Citing his own brother's eyewitness account, a narrator outlined what took place. Boyer was drunk, he said, and shot Goins six times with a .38 Special. As Boyer was walking away to reload his gun, the mortally wounded Goins opened his shirt to look at his wounds. He spent a week at home and was then transferred to the hospital, where he died a few days later.

The narrator commented that although Goins was unarmed at the time, "Somebody had to kill him. It didn't make much difference who done it, somebody had to kill him. He would get drunk and turn on his friends even." Boyer was indicted for killing Goins but won a "not guilty" verdict, thanks to a sharp defense lawyer and a body of witnesses who would not testify against him.

By the late 1930s, killings in the State Line country had slowed down. There were at least three other known killings during the decade, however, one of which was committed by a 17-year-old Brownsville youth during an argument and ensuing fight involving several of his friends and relatives. Easy-to-come-by whiskey was the chief factor in this and most other altercations in the study area during the years between the two world wars. Whiskey and rough behavior ushered in the era, and both were still much in evidence when the curtains were drawn on this event-filled period. Intensive agriculture, marked by hand cultivation, was still the mainstay of the area's economy, although logging and sawmilling continued— on a much reduced scale—to provide seasonal employment for some of the men. Perhaps the most marked change in the character of the State Line country by 1940 was the almost overnight disappearance of a bevy of familiar names from the warrant and indictment records. Questions to be raised in the next chapter include the reasons for the virtual disappearance of the familiar troublemakers and killers, and whether or not moonshining activities, brawling and other acts of public nuisance, and killing continued apace under new leadership and circumstances.

5

A New Generation

THE COMING of the modern era for the people of the State Line country was marked by the end of the Great Depression and the outbreak of World War II. Until that time, local economy, mores, codes of behavior, and churches and schools were all firmly rooted in the past. It was not a lack of propensity for change that characterized the culture; it was a lack of the wherewithal to move ahead. Modern conveniences that other Americans were beginning to accept as routine were not available to the people here. They did not yet have electricity in their homes, and that fact alone kept them tied to the old ways of doing things.

Further, the farm-to-market road program introduced by the Roosevelt administration did not alter the transportation scene in the study area. When the Depression ended, most families were still stranded on slick, muddy lanes throughout the winter months and whenever it rained in the summer; the best traveling was often in creek beds, which were lined with natural gravel. Given to the general lack of graveled and paved roads, automobiles remained rare throughout the 1930s. The few families fortunate enough to own a car or pickup truck would sometimes park it on or near the "good road," located up to three miles from the house, and walk out to it every week or two for a trip to town, hoping that the tires and battery would still be in running condition when they got there. As the family car was not yet the dangerous plaything that it came to be in this area by the later 1950s, transportation at the onset of the World War II was still accomplished largely on foot or horseback.

When modernization in the form of electricity, labor-saving devices, roads, consolidated schools, and (more recently) television satellite dishes finally came to the area, the people did avail themselves of such opportunities for advancement, but the forces of modernity were slow in coming. A questionnaire sent to 12 persons in April 1985, requesting information on "firsts" in their respective communities, elicited 11 responses. In the composite, the answers revealed that factory-made clothes were first available in the local stores between 1915 and 1920. These were largely men's and boys' shirts and overalls; women's ready-made dresses were yet to come. Factory-canned foods were introduced in the 1930s; prepackaged staples—rice, beans, sugar—came in the late 1930s and early 1940s. Most families still canned their own foodstuffs harvested from home gardens until the 1950s and 1960s, however. On the other hand, plow points, hoes, and other farm and garden implements had been sold at the local stores for as long as the respondents could remember, although local blacksmiths were called on to keep such items sharp and in good repair.

There were so few automobiles in the area in the 1920s that adults and children alike stood in doorways, gazed through windows, or peered over fences as the amazing contraptions laboriously negotiated the rough, unsurfaced roads that had been designed for horse-and-buggy travel. Most families who owned cars or pickup trucks did not acquire them until the early 1940s, and they did not become commonplace until 1948, a date that coincided with the advent of electricity for at least 80 percent of the State Line families. Farm tractors were even harder to come by, and their widespread ownership did not take place until the 1950s.

Available cash for most of the families before World War II came from the seasonal sale of a small patch of tobacco and a few head of hogs and cattle. Boys and girls made a little additional money for the purchase of personal items by digging yellowroot and ginseng roots, and by gathering apples and walnuts to sell to local merchants. The surest source of income for some of the families still came from moonshining and bootlegging, despite the fact that Prohibition had been gone for almost a decade. This was especially true on the Kentucky side of the line, where both counties were "bone dry" by virtue of local option. Logging and sawmilling, the third element in the area's tripartite economy after 1915, was greatly reduced in importance. The sawmills were generally relocated to the county seats by 1940, thus diminishing the possibility for State Line men to work there. In short, local industry was insufficient to integrate the study area into mainstream economy and culture by virtue of employment.

Despite the slow growth of forces that provide for the passing of provincialism, the geographical area of which the State Line country is a part was gradually being pulled into mainstream society by the late 1930s. It was at that time that packhorse libraries began to deliver books, newspapers, and magazines to some of the people living in the more remote sections of the study area. Newspapers from other places carried news of World War II even before America entered that struggle; local weeklies also contained numerous references to the impending war. A Washington, Kentucky, paper announced in bold type in September 1939, "Poland Will Defend Warsaw to the Last," and "Fate of the Balkans Being Discussed in Russia." In early October, that same paper carried the headline, "Chamberlain Scorns Hitler's Peace Plan." By 1940, local people were reading blow-by-blow accounts of the European war in their weekly newspapers. The stark reality of America's potential entry into the conflict came in August 1940, when the national guard unit in Brake County was mobilized and ordered to Wisconsin to engage in "war games." If the State Line country had previously been isolated from the world at large, that would no longer be the case.

The first local draft for military service took place during the late fall of 1940. Brake County, for example, had a draft quota for one person. Twelve men quickly volunteered to fill the slot, however—one of them from a family of troublemakers in the State Line country. With this single exception, no names of former hell-raisers were found on the lists of those persons who entered military service; by that time most of them were too old, though several of their sons did serve. The total number of servicemen from the State Line country, combined with the number of people who migrated to midwestern cities in response to wartime industrial needs, weakened the once-prominent patterns of rowdy behavior and killings. Only two homicides occurred here between 1939 and 1950, indicating that the grip of homicidal behavior had been broken by the disruption of older cultural patterns.

Most of the outmigrants chose Northtown, Indiana, or some nearby newly emerging industrial center. The move to Northtown began as a trickle in the late 1920s, continued apace through the 1930s, then became a swollen, almost turbulent stream during and after World War II. Local people who were too old for military service, or who were deferred because of the essential nature of their employment to the war effort, were already in Northtown when the war ended. Many returning military veterans chose to cast their lot with these former neighbors rather than go home to a farm in the State Line country that offered little more than a subsistence way of life.

At least 40 local families sent emigrants to Northtown. On the basis of oral interviews and of research in both Northtown's police records and the files of State Line newspapers—which almost weekly contained news sections called the "Northtown Letter"—a conservative estimate would fix the number of former State Line residents in this booming east central Indiana city at approximately 125 persons. By the late 1940s, there were enough people in Northtown from all over the four counties in which the study area is located that a columnist for the evening paper there wrote about the "numerous social goings and comings between Jessetown and Northtown." Perhaps with tongue in cheek, he proposed that the two places be designated "sister cities, or at least cousins"; he further suggested that the Northtown Chamber of Commerce should organize an official junket to Jessetown and "the surrounding areas in Kentucky" for the purpose of cementing this relationship.

Migrants from the study area worked at various jobs in

Northtown, but one particular factory stands out as the work-place choice to these southerners, and people back home in Kentucky and Tennessee came to recognize the name of that manufacturer more quickly than they recognized the name of the town itself. One story has it that when a bus bound for Northtown from the Jessetown area arrived in the city, the driver yelled out, "Northtown, Northtown," but none of the sleepy-eyed passengers made a move to get out of their seats. Suspecting that they were all going to work at the factory in question, the driver drove by the plant, then yelled out its name. The passengers immediately woke up, grabbed their satchels, and bounded from the bus.

Another story making the rounds among former State Line residents in Northtown indicates how the southerners them-selves perceived the vastness of their numbers. It seems that a northerner on the assembly line at the factory asked one of the migrants where he was from.

"Tennessee" was the prompt reply.

Assuming that all Tennesseans were from Jessetown, the first man spontaneously asked, "What part of Jessetown are you from?"

The narrator who told the anecdote then added, "See, up there they thought that Jessetown was a bi-i-i-g place."

In order to test the thesis held by some social scientists that southerners moving to new geographical areas and social set-tings around the country take with them the disposition for violent behavior,[1] it seemed appropriate to analyze the crimi-nal behavior of former State Line people residing in North-town after the war, along with the behavior of their offspring who were born there in the city. I contacted the Records Divi-sion of the Northtown Police Department and was provided with information on arrests and citations relevant to 28 family names and numerous given names of former troublemaking families. This search turned up 170 police records relative to those surnames, and I was able to identify 76 individuals whose names I had encountered previously in the study area; or whose place of birth, when given, was in the State Line country; or who, even though much younger and born in Northtown, could be readily identified by a combination of familiar given and last names. Moreover, all persons selected for analysis lived in what a captain in the Records Division identified as the part of town occupied by people of southern extraction.

Northtown police files for the 1940s, though incomplete, indicated that former State Line country residents were almost never involved in situations that called for police action: only two assault-and-battery charges and two traffic violations were recorded against them during those years. All four of these counts were against members of the original migrant generation; no children born to them in Northtown were arrested or cited for any purpose. In the 1950s only one assault-and-battery charge was recorded against the urban-born generation. The migrant generation had a slightly stepped-up police record for that decade, however, with 27 arrests or citations chalked up against them. The 1960s witnessed a greatly accelerated arrest/citation rate of both the migrants and their children born in the city. It should be noted, however, that many of the offenses in the various infraction categories were committed by the same persons; for example, someone stopped for drunken driving was generally charged with speeding or reckless driving, driving a faulty vehicle, having no operator's license, and—sometimes—resisting arrest. Thus, the total number of individual violators was relatively small at all times. Offenses by the first-generation migrants from the State Line country dropped considerably during the 1970s but during that decade their children and some grandchildren broke the law more frequently than they had during the 1960s. Records for the period 1980-84 revealed a significant drop in crime among both the migrant and city-born generations.

Most of the recorded violations fell into three major categories: improper vehicle handling (driving under the influence, speeding, reckless driving, no operator's license), noncriminal disorderly conduct, and alcohol possession. Relatively few criminal charges of lethal potential—carrying a gun without a permit (10 times), theft or burglary or breaking-and-entering (14), and armed robbery (2)—were brought against these people. Even these numbers are minimized by the fact that only five persons were responsible for all of the serious violations. The nearest that any of the migrants or their offspring ever came to committing a homicidal act occurred in 1982, when a woman born in Northtown to State Line parents was arrested and charged on two counts of attempted murder.

Here, then, is one group of southern migrants who did not carry with them the tendency for homicidal behavior that has been attributed to southerners everywhere in their new locations. The move from their violence-prone rural culture to alien city environs was apparently sufficient within itself to break the fatal code of behavior that had characterized their homeland since the years following the Civil War. Speaking in favorable terms for all of the migrants from the larger four-county area of which the study area is a part, a Northtown police captain commented, "They moved up here and worked at [the factory] in the late '30s and '40s, made some money, and changed their patterns of living." There is every indication that adaptation to a different culture caused an altered mode of living and new norms of conformity for these people. It changed their perceptions of themselves in the process.

The situation at home in the State Line country also changed, however slowly. Only four boys and girls from the families represented by the 12 questionnaires went to high school before the outbreak of World War II. It was not until the war's end that high school attendance began to be viewed as the means of preparing for the future. Before that time most young people were compelled by parents, or felt a personal obligation, to stay away from high school; their proper station was seen as in the fields or around the house. A formal education beyond elementary school was still seriously questioned by many people, especially older adults and parents who did not have the few dollars it took to keep a child in school each year. Until the early 1940s many people here seriously felt that the truly important things of life could be taught at home under adult leadership and supervision. Girls could learn to cook, preserve foodstuffs, and care for babies and small children in preparation for their own marriages. Boys could learn how to plant, cultivate, and harvest field crops against the day their own families' livelihood would depend on such skills. Only the parents and young people with a vision of the change that lay just around the corner were willing to break from this mold. Toward that end, some parents saw to it, even at considerable personal sacrifice, that their children went on to school.

By the mid-1940s, between one-fourth and one-third of the students were choosing to go on to school beyond the eighth grade. School attendance had become compulsory to age 16, and most students dropped out at that point (though some of them would have preferred to go on). For a number of boys who otherwise might have quit school, the possibility of playing varsity sports acted as a magnet in pulling them away from the cornfields and into the schools. There is no real way to gauge the extent, if any, to which the potential for and actual participation in varsity athletics reduced the homicide rate. Nevertheless, the reality must be reckoned with: young men who might have been roaming the countryside at night and on weekends in search of hell-raising "fun" could now burn off nervous energy and frustration on the athletic floor or field. All high schools in the vicinity had basketball beginning in the 1930s, and Fountain County fielded the area's first football team in 1941. The other counties soon followed this lead. Whether the changed behavior should be credited to athletic programs, to new course offerings in social studies, or to a multiplicity of interrelated social factors, something helped the young people of the 1940s to understand that moonshine-whiskey consumption and gun possession were lethal concommitants that offered nothing to help them prepare for the future.

It was the young people who were born during the period from the late 1920s to about 1940 who made the decision to go on to high school in the hopes of improving their own lives and those of their future offspring. They were also the first young people fortunate enough to have access to automobiles, which became a reality after the war for virtually every family in the study area. Automobiles, however, posed a new problem for State Line culture—death at the wheel.

Given the high local death rate caused by automobile accidents throughout the 1950s and 1960s, one might question whether the former inclination to violent behavior had really changed at all, or had simply been rechanneled through the ownership and use of automobiles. Headlines in local newspapers frequently announced the bloody accidents: "Three Die in Six Weeks," "Two Teen-Agers Die in Fiery Crash," "10 People Hospitalized in Head-On Collision," "Youth Killed When the Car He Was Driving at a High Rate of Speed Went out of Control on a Curve," "Six Persons Were Hospitalized Sunday When Their Car Failed to Make a Curve and Crashed Over a Culvert at Mattis." During one four-week period in 1963, a local newspaper carried news of a fatal accident each week. The highway death rate can easily be accounted for on the grounds that automobiles were basically new toys for these young people who, while frequently drunk or drinking, operated them at extremely high speeds over crooked roads whose danger-fraught courses had been carved out decades before cars were invented.

But although the automobile has become instrumental in numerous deaths within recent years, the State Line country has not been immune to occasional homicides and frequent demonstrations of lawlessness, reminiscent of older times, by a few young men in the area. The first killing to occur here after 1939 took place in January 1945, one mile west of the State Line country. According to the entry in a neighbor's diary, "Thomas Butts shot and killed a Mr. Bates, Thomas's son-in-law, on Boyer Mountain, January 1, 1945." Although slightly outside the study area, the shooting death of Bates is included here because it was descibed by a half-dozen narrators, indicating cultural proximity and affinity for the area and persons involved. Bates, the victim, was a man in his mid-60s. He was married to a much younger woman who was reportedly unfaithful to him; in fact, it was claimed by some that the other man gave Butts $100 to kill Bates. The actual shooting was provoked by Bates himself. He had gone to the Butts home to persuade his estranged wife to return home with him. When he threatened her with a gun, he was shot and killed by her father, who fired at him from a nearby window. Butts walked to the home of a neighbor and asked them to call the sheriff in Shelltown. He was subsequently tried for murder and acquitted. His widowed daughter remarried soon thereafter and moved out of the area.

The only other homicidal death in the 1940s occurred on August 16, 1947, just over the state line in the Hat Hollow locality. Elijah Coffelt shot and killed his 21-year-old nephew, reputedly over a woman whose favors they both sought. It was said that both men had been drinking. Coffelt went to Washington, Kentucky, and surrendered to the police. He was subsequently convicted of murder and sentenced to life in the penitentiary in November 1947.

The only killing that took place in the study area in the 1950s occurred in the Bear River Valley on the morning of August 3, 1950, as a murder-suicide, when Carl Haley shot and killed his estranged wife and then turned the gun on himself. The woman was on her way to vote (some say with a baby in her arms), along with her mother, brother, and sister, when Haley stepped out of the bushes with a sawed-off shotgun. The blast from the gun struck her in the head, killing her instantly. The man took a few steps backward, and fired once again, and crumpled over dead from a self-inflicted wound. A motive for the double shooting was never established, although sources close to the situation thought that the tragedy resulted from domestic tensions.

Sixteen months later, in January, 1952, four young men from the Bear River Valley were involved in what the local newspaper described as "a blazing gun battle with lawmen" on the streets of Jessetown. The four, none of whom had the same surnames as the pre–World War II hell-raisers, "were driving an automobile back and forth through town, drinking beer and throwing the bottles in the streets." When the sheriff and a deputy confronted them at a service station in town, one of the four men emerged from the car carrying a cocked shotgun. A companion, with hand in pocket, dared the two lawmen to go for their guns.

The sheriff reportedly told the two, "I know I'll burn for it, but I'll get one of you."

In the shootout that followed, the fellow with the concealed hand was killed, but the other three escaped.

Both the sheriff and deputy were tried for murder before a standing-room-only crowd, but were freed on a "not guilty" verdict. There was "no disturbance" by those present that day in court in May 1952. The sheriff's wife was shot from ambush 13 months later, however, while driving his car to Mattis to get eggs and produce for the county jail. The newspaper reported that her attackers "apparently thought that the sheriff was driving the car." She was wounded by two shots from a high-powered .351 rifle, and the car was hit five times.

Only one killing occurred during the 1960s, but it was not classified as a homicide and no jury trial was held. The event, which took place November 29, 1961, claimed the life of a sleeping man. His wife, Lotta Pomeroy, had prepared breakfast for her family that morning. Instead of calling them to the table as usual, she took down a shotgun from the wall, went to the side of her sleeping husband, and shot "the top of his head off." Their 16-year-old son told authorities that he saw his mother come from the victim's room with the gun. He removed the weapon from her hands and took it, along with two other guns found in their Bear River home, to his brother's home nearby. Lotta was apprehended about 200 yards from the house, wandering in a daze with ice frozen in her hair. With full support from her family, she was taken to the hospital in Jessetown and treated for shock. Later, she was committed to a mental institution for therapy.

The first violent death among members of the rowdy element since the late 1930s occurred on October 21, 1971, when

Arvil Christie shot and killed his brother, Hank; both were members of the same extended Honey Creek family that had been involved in a sizable number of altercations and killings across the years. A former sheriff recalled that he "had all sorts of trouble with the two brothers, running them, catching them every weekend, putting them in jail. They was into something all the time." A narrator explained why Arvil and Hank eventually turned on each other and what happened as a consequence.

One of them [Arvil] finally got married and he got jealous of the other one. So they was out 200-300 yards from where they lived on the highway that goes across the mountain there. And this older one—the one that was married—was jealous of the younger one. He told him he was going to kill him. And they had a few words about what it was all about, you know, and why he wanted to kill him. He accused him of fooling with his wife. And the other one denied it.

Well, this boy had his .22 rifle and the younger one [Hank] started to run, and did run until he was shot down by [the older brother, who was] loading and shooting as fast as he could load and shoot it. He shot him down and him running from him. Hit him two or three times with a .22 bullet. Killed him dead right there in the road.

And they never was nothing said or done about that.

Ten weeks later, on January 1, 1973, Balm Christie, a cousin of the two brothers, shot and killed his wife at his home between Mattis and Bell Fort. He had a long record dating from the early 1960s of charges for assault and battery, breaking and entering, and larceny. His past actions may have contributed to the shooting of his wife, as it was said that the event resulted from tensions at home, created by pressures exerted by one or more of his in-laws. Christie was tried and sent to prison.

On September 4, 1975, across the line at Tall Rock, 33-year-old Winford Coffelt also drew upon older culture patterns. It is reported that he got drunk and went home, allegedly intending to kill his wife. Her brother, Alvis Tarter, was there and was wounded during the initial round of shots. When Tarter fell over a chair, his son, who was also present, shot Coffelt. Both father and son then fired at Coffelt. Which one killed him was not determined with certainty, but that did not appear to matter to local officials; they held Alvis Tarter for "only one night in jail" before releasing him. One narrator said flatly, "And that was all there was to it."

The Coffelt-Tarter trouble simmered for about nine years, marked only by occasional verbal confrontations, and culminated on June 24, 1984, in what a Brake County jury ruled a double killing and homicide on the outskirts of Washington. Sammy Tarter, 75, the son of moonshiner Bing Tarter, who was gunned down in 1933 by a deputy sheriff and associates (see Chapter 4), shot and killed Bertram Coffelt (brother of Winfred Coffelt, above), 64, and Bertram's son Curtis, 37, over a disputed boundary line and other unproved allegations. The two older men were brothers-in-law. It was reported that the two Coffelts were hit between 12 and 20 times by blasts from Tarter's shotgun. Police arrived on the scene only minutes later. Tarter fled to avoid arrest, exchanging shots with the police as he ran. He died from a gunshot wound to the head, and—considerable public opinion to the contrary—the jury decreed that he himself fired the bullet that took his life.

This triple tragedy, described in the local paper as "the most nauseating thing" ever to occur in Brake County, shocked the entire area. But the reverberations did not produce as much anti-police sentiment among the people of the State Line country as the 1979 FBI ambush of Alvis R. Bartley when he left his mother's home in Bear River Valley under cover of darkness. That story assumed epic proportions and made a folk hero of Bartley who, by all official descriptions, was a hardened criminal.

Bartley was born in the Bear River Valley on July 12, 1934. People who knew him as a teenager recalled that he was a "good boy" who, according to a local newspaper, "wouldn't even drink a beer. He just loved to ride a motorcycle and never bothered anybody." Local folk at that time believed that Bartley would become a minister; some said he did preach a little at about age 18. The writer of one of the local newspaper accounts at Bartley's death presented a philosophical view of a life gone wrong: "What," the writer asked rhetorically, "made this man's life end up so different from others?" Providing his own answer, the journalist continued, "Somewhere along the way something happened. Maybe it was several things that happened to cause his life to change and end the way it did."

Whatever the precipitating factors, violence marked the turbulent life of Alvis D. Bartley. He was simultaneously placed on the FBI's list of Ten Most Wanted Fugitives and made a folk hero by friends and acquaintances in the State Line country. The first report of Bartley's disorderly behavior was gleaned from newspaper files of June 1959. With two companions, all in their mid-20s, Bartley was arrested and jailed in Jessetown for shooting a pistol and shotgun into a Methodist church in Bear River Valley. The three were also charged with beating up and shooting at the operator of a drive-in theater that same night.

During the next two to three years Bartley reportedly committed crimes in California, Indiana, Ohio, and Kentucky, and was wanted in those states as an armed robbery suspect. By then, he was credited with numerous jail escapes, and stories about his exploits and his boasts that no jail could hold him were making the rounds among local law officers and the general public.

His first shoot-out with law enforcement officials came in October 1962, when, in an attempt to avoid arrest, he flashed a .38 Special and fired at local authorities and two state troopers in Jessetown. He shot and injured one of the troopers before an officer's bullet grazed his head. Two additional shots from the trooper's gun hit Bartley in the stomach and left him partially but permanently paralyzed. From that time on, he wore braces on both legs and used a walking aid as well.

In January 1963, Bartley was sentenced to two separate five-year terms in the state prison at Nashville for wounding one of the troopers and firing at the other with intent to kill. The paralyzed "desperado," the newspaper called him, was carried smiling into the courtroom in Jessetown to hear the sentence pronounced. Although denied parole in late 1964, Bartley was released in 1966 and went at that time to Northtown, Indiana. But encounters with the police there prompted an Indiana judge to give him a suspended sentence on the provision that he never return to Indiana. Back home in Tennessee, he was almost immediately involved in a shoot-out with the sheriff and deputy sheriff of Fountain County. In January 1967, Bartley was sentenced to two consecutive seven-year prison terms on two counts of wounding and attempting murder. At the time of sentencing, he was awaiting trial on separate charges of assault and battery and armed robbery.

Bartley was again paroled, this time with instructions to leave Tennessee. He secretly returned to Northtown in 1970 and found employment as a gas station attendant. For unexplained reasons he pulled a gun on a customer, who reported the incident to the Northtown police, and Bartley was again arrested. Having both threatened the customer with a gun and violated his Indiana parole, he was sentenced 10 to 25 years in the state prison.

Paroled early once more, Bartley returned to Tennessee, where he was arrested in late December 1973 for allegedly shooting a deputy sheriff in Morgan County. The next August, Bartley and a fellow inmate escaped jail by worming through an 18-inch hole sawed through a metal plate. Following that escape, the FBI placed Bartley's name on its "most wanted" list in January, 1975. Dubbed "the mountain man" by federal agents, he was sought for unlawful flight to avoid prosecution, attempted first degree murder, bank robbery, and attempted burglary. Through the aid of family and friends and because of his intimate knowledge of the mountainous terrain surrounding his Bear River home, Bartley "scouted around" and managed to avoid detection and arrest for nearly five years—even though the FBI reportedly had as many as 50 agents assigned to capture him.

The unwanted presence of the federal agents, coupled with their abrasive tactics in dealing with local citizens suspected of aiding and abetting Bartley, was a constant source of irritation to people in the State Line country. One narrator articulated the attitude toward the FBI held by most residents: "When the FBI wants you, they don't want you alive. They'd rather have you dead." The presence of federal agents strengthened the determination of local people to shield and care for their new-found hero as long as necessary. Several narrators told of the verbal and physical abuse they experienced at the hands of federal men and the local law enforcement officials who assisted them in their search for Bartley during the five-year period. One narrator from Honey Creek told of his outright defiance of some officers from the Tennessee Bureau of Investigation:

There's some TBI men come here one time and called me out on the porch about Alvis Bartley and asked me if I'd feed him.

I said, "If he was hungry, I'd give it to him. But I wouldn't harbor him."

He said, "That would be harboring him."

I said, "I don't give a goddam what it would be. That's what I'd do. Wouldn't you?"

He studied a little while, then said, "I don't know whether I would or not."

Three narrators from Brake County teamed up in 1982 to describe their attitudes toward the FBI and their encounters with its agents while Bartley was in hiding:

Narrator A: I'll bet that Alvis R. Bartley stayed in my old house on the mountain back there for over two years. I never seen him, but there were piles of pork-and-beans cans. And the old house had a good fireplace. It was a log cabin—sealed and weatherboarded.

Narrator B: The people who knowed Alvis R. Bartley said he was a good fellow. He got in there [on the wrong side of the law], and there was no way for him to get out.

Narrator A: They got him on the run and he had to do things when they got him that way.

Narrator B: A person in Jessetown told me that the deputy that they claimed Bartley shot at, had took his [Bartley's] wife. And I've had my brother say to me that if Bartley ever come down here to be good to him. Said he wouldn't harm a thing.

Narrator A: [Laughing] The FBI *stayed* with me and him [Narrator B] there.

Narrator B: I was mowing out here next to the garage and had my back turned, and one of them bumped me! Walked right up against me! He was with the sheriff from Worley. I turned around and said, "Get that gun back! I'm nervous." The sheriff from this county told him, "You'd better get that gun down." I said, "I ain't done nothing and I ain't going to be bothered." He said, "We ain't going to bother you." He handed me some papers with this picture. I said, "I don't know him. I've heard of him, but wouldn't know him if I was to run up on him."

Narrator C: One FBI man asked me would I feed him if he came here. I said, "Yes, I'd feed him!"

Narrator A: They asked me the same thing, and I said, "I sure would!" They said, "Why would you?" "Well," I said, "I never turned nobody down anyway, and if he's as bad of a man as they say he is, I'd be afraid to deny him." [Laughter]

At the time of his death, Bartley had been holed up in a cave near the Fountain-Trundle county line, almost a mile from the nearest road. The entrance to the cave was located about half-way up the side of the hill, and "could not be seen any further away than approximately 15 feet, as it resembled a rock out-cropping similar to many others in the area." The opening was less than three feet in diameter, but there was a 20-foot vertical drop just inside a small chamber in which Bartley had constructed a living area with scrap lumber, strings, rubber inner tubes, plastic bags, and small saplings used for a bed. He had devised systems for channeling water into the cave, for disposing of waste materials, and for storing such items as meal, flour, oatmeal, and bullets in glass containers in an effort to keep out moisture. The fugitive had kept an accurate record of the passage of time by crossing out the days on a calendar one at a time.

Bartley was a gifted artist, as demonstrated by his numerous oil paintings depicting religious personalities and scenes, which still adorn some homes and churches in the Bear River Valley. Paint and brushes were found inside his cave home, but no paintings were discovered by authorities; it was assumed that he did not keep them in the damp cave for long, lest they be permanently damaged.

Death came to Bartley a few days short of age 45, on July 7, 1979, ending the five-year FBI search. Numerous federal and state agents, accompanied by local lawmen, were staked out in the field near the home of Bartley's 75-year-old mother on the weekend of July 4, hoping that he might decide to visit her sometime during the holiday. He did. Then, shortly after midnight, he left his mother and started back across the field to his cave. When he ignored a shouted order to surrender, two quick shots fired by an FBI agent ended the turbulent life of this outlaw who was eulogized as "a good old country boy who would give you the shirt off of his back."

"While law enforcement officials considered Bartley a dangerous fugitive," wrote the editor of a local paper, "the people of Bell Fort who knew him [best] thought of him as something different. . . . He had become quite a folk hero to the people of the mountains near where he was born, lived and died." Three years later, on the anniversary of his death, a memorial tribute was published in that same newspaper: a printed message of bereavement under a photograph of Bartley posing with one of his religious paintings. It ended with the words, "You are missed and loved by your family and friends. Alvis, we love you."

While it would be easy to choose sides for or against Bartley, the real significance of his outlaw life rests in the manner in which it reflects local attitudes toward "criminal" activity and the formal system of law enforcement. His turbulent career and "needless" death ("He never killed anybody") epitomize the past and present attitudes exhibited by residents of the State Line country against interference by intrusive and unwelcome law enforcement officials.

Conclusion

I began this investigation of killings in the State Line country because I suspected that the homicide rate there was higher than in the surrounding region; I wanted to determine whether that was indeed the case and, if so, why. Once narrators understood my purpose and accepted me, I was struck by the candor with which they talked about the numerous fatal episodes that had taken place in their home communities. Equally impressive were their attitudes of acceptance toward these killings. The narrators did not view most of the homicides, regardless of the motive, as criminal acts. In this, their definition of crime differed markedly from that established by statute and enforced by local officers.[1] They viewed the killers as law-abiding, moral beings, not unlike other area residents, and people looked upon violent behavior in a matter-of-fact way. As one student of the South has said, it was "an essential fact of human life somehow built into human relationships."[2] For these reasons, it may be hypothesized that the State Line country was, and perhaps still is, a subregional culture that tolerated violence in all forms, including homicide.

Demonstrating the existence of this regional culture of violence in the study area calls for analysis of its key features, along with the historical factors that gave birth to and fostered it. Having examined the nature of the violence in this light, we can then place the State Line country and its killings in larger regional and national perspective and, in so doing, offer a critique of the existing scholarship on southern homicidal traits and of the generally accepted scholarly position that the South as a whole is a regional culture of violence.

A look at homicide statistics for the study area affords a good starting place for such an analysis. The table indicates the number of homicides in the study area (excluding those directly engendered by the Civil War) by five-year periods from 1850 to 1979. The years from 1885 to 1915 were marked by a fairly high but almost steady rate of killings. A noticeable jump occurred following 1915, however, as the introduction of saw-milling and the traffic in illegal whiskey were beginning to change the character of local culture. Thus, the decade of the 1920s witnessed a substantial increase in the number of killings over the previous decade, from 9 to 14, and the number remained high during the first years of the 1930s, until shifts in the area's economy—most noticeably in outmigration—produced a corresponding change in the culture of the State Line country. What the raw numbers tell us, first of all, is that violence apparently began after the Civil War and, second, that it was heavily influenced by changes in the local economy. Beyond this recounting, however, lie the features of the killings themselves which, upon analysis, reveal something of the local definition of crime and the limits placed on violence as acceptable behavior. I am referring to who did the killings, the situations in which they took place, the motives behind them, the relationships of the people involved, the attendant factors in each case (e.g., the prevalence of deadly weapons and alcohol), and local attitudes toward law enforcement officers and the courts. A consideration of these features follows.

In this society in which men dominated the community's public life, acts of homicide involved male against male with only three or four exceptions. Beyond the homicide episodes described here, male behavior was totally acceptable by mainstream society's standards. Although many of the men engaged in hell-raising, it was typically just loud and boisterous, not physically abusive and violent. I did not record a single instance of child abuse; furthermore, I was told of only two or three episodes of physical abuse between husband and wife. Thus, without exhibiting violent behavior in daily activities, men often used killing as a legitimate means of settling serious

Number of Non–Civil War Killings per Five-Year Period,
1850-1979

Years	Number of Killings	Years	Number of Killings	Years	Number of Killings
1850-54	0	1895-99	2	1940-44	0
1855-59	1	1900-04	3	1945-49	2
1860-64	0	1905-09	3	1950-54	1
1865-69	3	1910-14	2	1955-59	0
1870-74	0	1915-19	7	1960-64	0
1875-79	1	1920-24	6	1965-69	0
1880-84	1	1925-29	8	1970-74	2
1885-89	4	1930-34	8	1975-79	1
1890-94	3	1935-39	4		

disputes. Somehow, this culturally inculcated fatal code became a functioning part of their existence.

The four types of situations in which non–Civil War related
homicides were committed included *confrontation*, in which
the victim interacted with, or at least saw, the killer just before
death occurred; *ambush*, or clandestine killings in which the
victim was unaware of immediately impending death; *brawl or
fight*, involving the introduction of a lethal weapon into a
spontaneous altercation; and *miscellaneous*, including unknown or undetailed circumstances (see Figure 1).

Confrontations accounted for over half of the deaths. The
victim and assailant in this situation knew and typically bore
ill-will toward each other. Aware that their culture generally
expected them to settle interpersonal disputes directly, they
anticipated the possibility of death in the event of a face-to-
face encounter. The fact that the majority of the killings occurred as the result of confrontation demonstrates that this
was, in fact, an accepted and even expected course of events.
The large number of attacks from ambush (35 percent of the
homicides) is thus one of the real surprises of this study. It can
perhaps be explained in terms of the motives for the bush-

whackings which included seeking revenge for rape or theft, or settlement of a prior disagreement. Only 9.5 percent of the ambushings were related to whiskey traffic or consumption, thus indicating that the perpetrators in these instances were resolute, strongly motivated individuals who were mentally prepared to kill without alcoholic fortification but who were afraid to risk meeting their enemies openly. The remaining deaths (11 percent) were equally divided between the brawling and miscellaneous categories.

Whether the killings were of the premeditated or heat-of-passion variety seemed not to matter to residents of the study area; they made no distinction between deliberate and spontaneous homicide in their acceptance of the deaths and the attitudes expressed toward them. Evidently, the community code of violence held that even willful, premeditated killings were justifiable, given the proper set of circumstances.

Among motives for the killings (see Figure 2), protection of property accounted for approximately one third. The circumstances involved in this category included boundary line disputes, rival moonshining operations, robberies, thefts, arguments over debts, estate settlement disputes, and land purchases. Domestic quarrels alone, without regard for economic or other ulterior motives, prompted 23 percent of the pre-1940 killings, while revenge ran a close second with 19 percent. Disagreements from unspecified causes (12.5 percent), drunken altercations (8 percent), avoidance of arrest (4 percent), and paid manslaughter (2 percent) complete the list of classifiable motives. The reasons did not change appreciably from the 1880s to 1940, and killings consistently took place under similar sets of circumstances and in strikingly analogous ways. Even the ones that occurred in the logging and sawmilling camp environment (14.5 percent) were performed in ways familiar and understandable to local residents.

In some instances the assailant may have been driven to the murder as much by the victim's own psychological or symbolic aggression as by personal inclination. In other words, the victim may have provoked the homicide by intentionally caus-

Figure 1. Homicidal Situations, 1880-1939

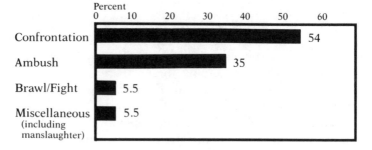

Figure 2. Classifiable Motives for Killings, 1880-1939

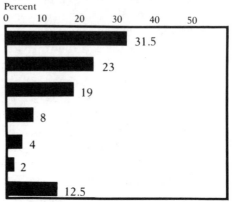

Figure 3. Relationships of Killers and Victims, 1880-1939

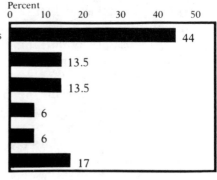

ing the killer to suffer grief, anxiety, or anguish through non-violent means or through the use of obscene or abusive language. This type of provocation is closely related to what Marvin E. Wolfgang has termed "victim-precipitated" homicide, which commonly occurs between two people who know each other well and are all too familiar with each other's personality and character traits.[3] Homicides resulting from symbolic aggression appear to have been fairly common in the study area, although this assumption is based solely on the recorded oral accounts of area residents. By way of illustration, recall that one victim had kicked the killer's dog, and another had called his killer "a damned hog thief." The motives for most of the killings clearly reveal that homicides functioned in defense of home, property, and personal honor.

A look at the relationships between killers and victims (see Figure 3) reveals that, typical of southern homicides as a whole,[4] lethal violence in the study area between friends and/or neighbors accounted for 44 percent of the homicidal deaths from the 1880s to 1940. Domestic killings between in-laws, cousins, siblings, parents and children, and spouses, in that order, together accounted for an additional 27 percent of the homicides, with killings among blood relatives and those related only through marriage divided equally. In addition to familial homicides, the killer-victim relationships also included romantic triangles (6 percent) and fellow workers (6 percent); 17 percent took place between persons of unknown relationships. The fact that the majority of the killings involved people who knew each other well indicates that the accepted code of violence was strong enough to override the ties of family and friendship.

Two attendant factors in most of the killings—factors that constituted powerful influences in the perpetuation of violence in the study area—were the high value placed on the ownership and display of guns and the ready availability and widespread use of alcohol. Every family had one or more guns in the house for shooting rodents, snakes, domestic meat animals, and wild game, and most men regularly carried weapons concealed on their persons. They knew how to use them and, in the company of alcohol, often did. Whether alcohol induced violent behavior directly, or whether it acted as what Sarnoff A. Mednick calls a "disinhibitor of preexisting aggressive tendencies" is not known.[5] One way or another, however, whiskey prepared the men to resort to guns, which might have gone unused had their owners been sober. State Line males apparently got quite a boost from three or four big "swigs" of moonshine whiskey straight from the jar, coupled with the feel of gun metal in their hip pockets or tucked under their belts. With these two lethal factors at work, a shooting resulted from virtually any confrontation among these fellows. Whiskey figured in 94 percent of the killings, either through production or consumption, and the gun was employed as the instrument of death in over 90 percent of them. Usually, both killer and victim had been drinking just prior to the argument that produced the killing.

The final feature of the killings in the State Line country to be examined is their relationship to the law enforcement system. Many killings went unreported to the authorities at the time. Attending physicians here (and probably elsewhere as well) circumvented the possibility of being involved in court hearings by not indicating the likelihood of felonious assault on the victim's death certificate.[6] (This accounts for the fact that the homicide rate for the study area far exceeds the number reported by Harrington C. Brearley[7] for the total of the four counties, even though the area is no more than one-tenth the combined size of the four counties.) As a result, most of the homicides here went unpunished in the courts through the 1920s.

Lax or corrupt methods of law enforcement and a strong feeling that justice was seldom done in the courts were also factors in the lack of reporting of killings. Narrators felt that some sheriffs and deputies could be bought off with a little cash or a few bottles of whiskey, and cited instances in evidence. (The officers they trusted most were those who had once trafficked in whiskey themselves—and the number was fairly large.) People who could not afford the services of a good lawyer could not expect to receive equitable and fair treatment in a court of law. And when persons charged with killing were brought to trial, partisan politics and intimidation were brought to bear upon witnesses, who were terrified and generally unwilling to testify truthfully.

Horace Redfield's conclusions about unpunished murder in the South of 1870 were and still are relevant to the court systems that have jurisdiction over the State Line country. He astutely observed that, if arrested, a murderer was unlikely to be convicted because the jurors themselves had often been personally involved in violent acts and might be again, and feared that a relative or friend of the accused might sit on their own juries in the future. Moreover, there was always the possibility of retaliation by the family of the accused. Finally, such murders were frequently committed for reasons the jurors approved and considered justifiable.[8] Texas law, for example, exonerated a killer who acted under an "irresistible influence" to commit homicide.[9] Southern jurors were not then and are not now inclined to prejudge people accused of an act of violence.

Largely because of the area's physical isolation and political fragmentation among four counties, there was a general absence of effective law enforcement through the 1930s. Residents of the State Line country of necessity, then, established an internal system for determining motives and therefore culpability for the killings. The folk system of justice that developed was a community-based inquest that called for an on-the-spot determination not of guilt or innocence but of motive. As killing was considered to be a local matter, county authorities were infrequently called in to investigate. A former sheriff told me that during his tenure of office in the 1950s, three murders were committed and burials accomplished without his being immediately notified of the deaths. The inquest system, which produced no formal papers for the record, was designed to establish the justifiability of the killer's action. If the explanation was "right" in the eyes of the neighbors, who generally viewed killing as a response to a precipitating factor, the matter was settled for all time, and the killer was exonerated and reintegrated into the group.[10] Thus, the main function of the early community inquests was one of maintaining order, not enforcing the law in the strict sense. Viewed in this light, these inquests were extremely successful: the community was in control of "due process"; its members registered satisfaction with the outcome; and social order and cultural stability were maintained.[11] Only when improved roads in the 1930s and 1940s permitted easier access to the sites of the killings by the sheriff or a deputy and by an attending physician who had to pronounce the victim legally dead did the community inquest slowly fade from the scene.

Responses to my pointed questions revealed only two categories of crime that the community defined as lawless behavior. These were rape, and killing a neighbor during a robbery or theft. Both were committed by the very few "hardened" criminals who were considered amoral; their willful acts of aggressive violence were of such an unacceptable nature that they fell well beyond the bounds of community legitimation. Both categories were viewed as punishable with the full force of constituted law. In 1929 a local man, in company with his brother and a cousin, entered a local school, ran the children off, and raped the young teacher. The attacker was sentenced to be hanged in Washington but was pardoned by the governor. He has never been forgiven by the local people, however, who still become incensed when this incident of rape is mentioned. One person related with bitter contempt that the victim's uncle heard her screams as she was dragged from the schoolhouse but refused to go to her assistance. "If that had been my niece being raped," the narrator said through gritted teeth, "I'd have shot him like a dog."

The inexcusability of rape was again demonstrated in 1950 when a rapist being sought by a Brake County sheriff's posse was shot and killed in an area adjacent to the State Line country by a citizen of the community. When the latter was brought to trial, the local newspaper reported that "the not guilty verdict rendered by the jury in only twelve minutes was greeted by cheers by a large crowd in the courtroom." The newspaper defended the older folk code of justice by observing that "the trial should not have been held, [but since it was] all parties concerned should consider it completely settled and forget it as soon as possible."

State Line people also condoned and seemingly approved of the killing of certain thieves and robbers who stole for a living instead of working. The ambush slaying of Leon Billings, the reputed hog thief, illustrates this point (see Chapter 4). On the other hand, any person who killed another while committing a robbery or theft was less than human and guilty of wanton murder, as illustrated by the case of Bran Nesbitt, hired hand, who killed the Tunks during an attempt to rob them of cash recently gained from the sale of livestock (Chapter 1).

Local attitudes toward theft likely derived from pioneer times in the State Line country, when the prevailing system of justice here as elsewhere in the nation called for property protection above all other considerations. Human life ranked lower on the scale of social values. Individual effort and achievement were strongly encouraged, and property, both personal and real, was sought with zeal by the majority of residents. Once obtained, it was regarded as almost sacred, for the owners generally came by it only after years of hard work and frugal living. A person who had thus earned property, it was felt, should never lose it by theft or robbery to someone who chose to steal rather than do an honest day's work. Had anyone broken into the smokehouse of that nineteenth-century farmer who worried from year to year how he would raise the 60 cents necessary to pay his property taxes, and had the thief been shot and killed in the act (or even a few days later), the moral code of the State Line culture would have exonerated the farmer (owner) without a second thought. Further, the dead thief's family would have understood the violent retribution and forgiven the killer. Such community and family forgiveness was repeatedly illustrated in this study in connection with homicides resulting from various forms of thievery—

including boundary disputes, missing livestock—and from cases of rape.

Because the State Line country was historically isolated from law enforcement officials, and continued to be so through the 1930s, local residents were forced to assume responsibility for maintaining a stable social order as best they could. "Back then," commented a narrator, "you almost protected yourself." Another observed, "Through this country, you were your own law." Until the 1930s, most law officers were inconsistently viewed as being invariably present and intrusive "when they were not needed" yet seemingly never available on request, given distances sometimes in excess of 30 miles over nearly impassable roads.

As a logical outgrowth of the community's internally controlled system of law and order, shooting deaths committed by lawmen were especially despicable in the eyes of the local people. When law enforcement officials killed a person in what outsiders might consider to be the line of duty, local residents frequently had other thoughts on the matter. In such an event, the community held that even offenders with long criminal records were guiltless. The FBI's most-wanted Alvis D. Bartley, who was bushwacked in 1979 by combined federal, state, and local officers "in his mother's front yard" (Chapter 5), and moonshiner Bing Tarter, who was gunned down by a deputy sheriff for resisting arrest (Chapter 4), both died unnecessarily from the viewpoint of the people; they remain especially bitter over Bartley's death.

The fact that both men were guilty from a legal point of view and yet were exonerated by local public opinion raises two additional questions for which there are no ready answers. Was it their rather low socioeconomic stations in life that fixed public opinion in their favor? Or was it that their fates vicariously stirred the latent resistance of the area's population to governmental interference? Although guilty as charged, both men were elevated within the community to the status of wronged folk heroes after the lawmen had shot and killed them. Other offenders in the area such as Bunt Groce, the

Goinses, and Ernie Boyer (Chapter 4), who were not rich at the time they were involved in killings but financially well fixed in comparison with virtually all other local people, did not fare nearly as well when their actions were judged by the community. The question of vicarious resistance to government, regardless of the form it takes, may be answered in part by noting that there has long been a regional tradition of rebellion and cynicism toward governmental agencies and institutions.[12] This is nowhere better illustrated than in one of the local Congressional districts that reelected its incumbent in 1984 while he was still in federal prison in Alabama for failure to file his 1979 and 1980 federal income tax returns.

We have seen that the community's system of justice forgave the offender if the motive for the crime was justifiable in the community's eyes. Despite the criticism that might be leveled at such a system of justice, it effectively prevented needless retributive bloodshed by family members. Homicides were individual matters and thus did not develop into vendettas. Further proof that individuals within the culture were deemed responsible for their actions is indicated by the total failure of the narrators to use the word "blood" in describing family ties. The terms "blood kin," "blood brother," "blood ties"—in common usage elsewhere—were never employed, nor was the proverbial comparison "Blood is thicker than water." This observed absence in conversational references about kinfolk indicates that for the narrators, individuals rather than families constituted the basic units of society.[13] Kinship and family ties were important, but not to the point that relatives of the guilty parties were willing to take responsibility for the violent acts. In other words, persons who killed were personally responsible for their own actions. The fact that family members of the victims generally did not blame the killers or members of their families and, with only three exceptions, did not attempt to take revenge, indicates that individuals presumably understood the prescribed behavioral patterns and knew that they would be held personally accountable for their own deeds. This indicates that a rather surprising cultural code was at work: "We are not our brothers' keepers and thus are not responsible for their actions."[14]

To be fully understood, the fatal code of violence revealed in the foregoing constellation of features surrounding the killings must be set within the context of crucial elements in the State Line country's social and historical development. As stated in Chapter 1, the study area was populated by white Protestants, largely of British stock,[15] beginning about 1800 in the Bear River Valley. By and large, however, the rest of the area was not populated until 1830 and beyond. The period between 1830 and 1860 was critical in the formation of the area's culture—a time when people were establishing and developing social institutions, cultivating relationships with neighbors, and carving out ways of making a living. In 1860 the State Line country was, at most, only one generation removed from the frontier experience and therefore possessed a very fluid culture.

We have already seen that homicides did not occur in large numbers in the State Line country until the 1880s. Thus, in seeking a beginning point for the development of violent behavior in the area, we cannot point to antebellum dueling and the tense race relations caused by slavery.[16] Although there were 61 blacks in the Bear River Valley in 1860, official records and oral evidence do not mention any trouble between slaves and owners. Further, aristocratic duels and the violence they spawned in the lowland South were unheard of in this geographical area. Instead, the violence and resulting pattern of killings seem to stem from the critical juncture in the area's historical development—the coming of the Civil War. It was during those traumatic years that guerrilla activity in the State Line country pitted neighbor against neighbor, friend against friend, and relative against relative. Given the unchecked renegade activity during that strife-filled era, killings became common in the Bear River Valley, and earlier constraints against violence put into motion by the pioneer generation were now disregarded. The fact that the guerrilla activity occurred at a point when the area's cultural patterns were still impressionable seems to have permanently altered the character of local culture.

Justification for this argument lies in the fact that there is no evidence of any killings prior to 1858 in the study area. In the absence of formal records and newspapers from that era, the only information available about any early killings comes from oral tradition. Although the oral recollections that have been passed down from before the Civil War period are slim, existing traditions nevertheless attest to certain dramatic and sensational events and characters from frontier times, such as Indian removal, the notorious Harpes (later of Cave-in-Rock, Illinois, fame), and Davy Crockett, who lived for a brief time in the general vicinity of the State Line country. Because a body of oral legendry exists about these subjects, it is reasonable to assume that if killings had taken place prior to the Civil War, their sensational nature would have made them talked about in the same way that the postwar killings are.

The argument is bolstered by the fact that the grandparents of most of the narrators were born between 1840 and 1860. The father of one of them, in fact, was born in 1825 and lived until 1902, at which time the narrator was 12 years old. She commented to me, "My father and my grandmother on my mother's side used to talk about the old times, and I listened." But their talk, and that of other narrators in an area that relied on word-of-mouth news, did not include information about antebellum killings. The earliest killings discussed were those inflicted by guerrilla bands during the Civil War, suggesting that residents were unaccustomed to lethal violence prior to those years. Corroboration of this position is provided by the diary of Rev. A.B. Alford, which begins in 1844 but makes no mention of homicide in the Bear River Valley until 1858. The fact that he records the killing in that year at all indicates its extraordinary nature within the community.

The Civil War, during which approximately 36 residents of the Bear River Valley alone were brutally slain by neighbors and one-time friends, not only trained men to use guns in mortal conflict but also planted seeds of violence that sprouted and grew with each slaying both during and after the war.[17] To a lesser extent, the same process occurred in Waterfall, Little Piney Fork Valley, and in the Apple Bottom area two miles west of Tall Rock. A tendency for lethal violence in these valley settlements began by virtue of guerrilla warfare, spread across the adjacent countryside, and left a self-perpetuating imprint on local culture.

The fact that it was guerrilla activity and not the war itself that was the precipitating factor in the study area's subsequent violence is borne out by comparing the State Line country with my home community, located approximately 75 miles to the west. My home locale, if enclosed to contain the same number of square miles as the study area, witnessed approximately one-sixth as many homicides during the same period as that covered in this study. The two areas are culturally very similar, and their histories are much alike—with one very noticeable difference: although opposing armies criss-crossed the area, my community was not ravaged by guerrilla warfare during and after the Civil War. There was loud, boisterous behavior during the postwar years, and there was some theft and robbery, but only three known instances of homicide took place between 1865 and 1900, and just six additional killings occurred during the present century.

The violent tendencies generated by guerrilla activity in the study area during the war were aggravated in the 1870s by the imposition and attempted enforcement of a federal tax on distilled beverages. The effects of this measure were twofold. First, most people stopped making their own whiskey for domestic purposes and bought it from the few persons in the community who took to moonshining and made whiskey to sell. This meant in practice that men would gather at a moonshine outlet to drink. The result was rowdy behavior that frequently led to altercations and killings. Second, because the moonshiners flouted the law and the rest of the community encouraged them to do so, at least implicitly, respect for the law in general was undermined, and a disdainful attitude developed toward it and its officers.

The principle of property protection at all costs, mentioned earlier, carried by extension into the realm of moonshining and bootlegging. When a family's life savings had been spent in procuring moonshine equipment, that equipment was protected by the endemic folk code against federal and local law enforcement officials (viewed as legal thieves) as well as against local competitors in the whiskey business. In this moonshining culture, killing in protection of whiskey stills was acceptable, however marginally, to others in the area. Seen in the light of loyalty to the culture, one can understand why some local law officers refused to "rat" on the offenders, and why they often sent runners in advance of a federal raiding party to announce the approach.

The social institutions that were in the process of developing just before and after the Civil War did little to counteract the deleterious effects of both guerrilla warfare and illegal whiskey. The few and scattered part-time schools and churches had little influence on the character of the area through the 1930s.[18] It was not until that decade that the schools began to offer nine months of instruction each year. The length of the school term evolved over a period of many years, beginning back at the turn of the century, when they generally lasted only three months. These early schools were mainly concerned with teaching the basics, and in no readily discernible way did they attempt to address social issues. Students were sometimes introduced to moral and ethical teachings through the stories they read in their graded readers, but such books contained accounts of boys and girls in faraway places that were totally alien and unreal to the State Line children.[19]

In short, the grammar schools did little to help children reach out beyond their familiar surroundings to establish any connection between the local experience and the universal. Their world view extended no farther than the nearest community. How could these boys and girls know that moonshining was an illegal activity that promoted violence and other social ills when moonshine was made at home? (In two instances in the study area, schoolhouses themselves were used as places where whiskey was made during months that school was not in session). How could they know that killings were wrong when their own fathers, grandfathers, uncles, and neighbors had been involved in such happenings on one or more occasions?

Churches fared little better in creating social awareness in the community. The itinerant ministers who held forth once a month with hard-driving, fist-pounding, hellfire and damnation preaching—all intended to bring sinners to the altar of repentance—were generally successful in evangelical terms, it appears, as most of the people of the area were religious, even if not all of them were churchgoers. Sinners repented of their transgressions, sometimes year after year, but just what sins they had committed were never particularized. Ministers preached that sin was wrong, but they did not single out the types of behavior that were damaging the structure of the community. The main reasons why their sermons did not persuade people to leave their guns and alcohol at home is that while there was much sincere singing, shouting, and praising the Lord within the church, the ministers were not reaching those who needed to hear the Word proclaimed. The hard-core trouble makers were seldom, if ever, in attendance. Those persons present consisted mainly of women, children, and older men, while many of the husbands and fathers who "went to church" remained outside the building during worship services to talk about crops, weather, and other topics of community interest. Furthermore, some preachers had even made moonshine whiskey themselves; in one known instance, a Sunday School superintendent was also a bootlegger.

The chief stabilizing and shaping influence in the culture of the State Line country after the Civil War was the development of self-sufficient agriculture. By 1900, most people had sufficient land, livestock, equipment, and buildings to accommodate their everyday needs. Within a dozen years, however, the commercial sawmilling interests that had earlier ravaged the Appalachian uplands to the east bled over into the State Line country. The changes that sawmilling activities wrought were economically as well as ecologically irreversible, for they introduced wage employment to people who had previously realized little cash income.

Sawmilling thus brought a fundamental shift in the area's economic structure from agricultural self-sufficiency to paid labor, along with an increase in the supply of money and the things it could buy. Gambling and infrequent theft of money and goods were reported in the camps, as might have been expected, but there were no reports of killings resulting from these situational factors. The reasons for the high rate of homicidal activity in the milling camps cannot be explained apart from the fact that local men, who had grown to maturity in a culture that permitted killing to settle disputes, were now brought into close proximity, living and working within arm's reach of each other. Killing here was a response—although not one specifically articulated by the narrators—to social and economic tensions, heavy whiskey consumption, and seemingly minor altercations that readily blossomed into major ones.

During the depression years of the 1930s, the timber industry, along with other components of the local economy, suffered serious setbacks. Sawmilling camps closed down, forcing those who had become accustomed to steady wages to look outside the region for work. This search produced a substantial outmigration from the study area to totally new agricultural and industrial environments in the Midwest, and a consequent alteration in the culture of the State Line country, including a reduction in rowdy and violent behavior. There was a 30 percent decrease in local homicides during the last years of that decade, a reduction twice as great as that experienced nationally.[20] Thanks mainly to heavy out-migration, stepped-up efforts against moonshiners and other lawbreakers, military service in World War II, and a much higher rate of high school attendance, the local homicide rate had declined from 114 per 100,000 inhabitants in 1925 to only 10 in 1945. (Currently, in the 1980s, the rate hovers around 20, although this should not be viewed as a return to earlier patterns of behavior that produced a rate of killing four and five times as great.)

The homicides that occurred in the State Line country,

beginning in the 1880s and peaking in the 1930s, accurately reflected a series of upheavals in the area's cultural and social values. In the 1880s, violent tendencies engendered by the Civil War united with the unchecked flow of moonshine whiskey. In the 1910s, the introduction of a wage economy created a conflict with the existing system of self-sufficient agriculture that persisted through most of the 1930s. While only a very few residents were actually involved in the violence that resulted in homicide, everyone was affected in one way or another, as whiskey, fists, and guns reigned over the land from the 1880s into the 1930s. For the fifty-year period divided by the turn of the century, small irritants or threats to persons with rebellious, boisterous spirits and sharp tempers caused them to react violently with fists and, all too often, with lethal weapons. A drunken altercation in those days was almost always unrestrained and often ended in a killing. These acts of violence frequently occurred between friends (or former friends) and often over seemingly insignificant matters.

Although affected by social and economic conditions that varied with changing times, the pattern of violence in the State Line country derived ultimately from deep-rooted historical and cultural factors. Area residents seemingly learned from historical experience, and from cultural inculcation through imitation and modeling during childhood and early adult years, to accept killing as a means of settling disputes;[21] they seemingly permitted such acts as long as the culturally bound parameters were adhered to; they learned to live with the ever-present possibility that a member of their own family might be involved in homicide as killer or victim, depending on the situation; and they learned the art of forgiving the aggressor.

I have hypothesized that the State Line country may have produced a culture in which a code developed that permitted violence as an acceptable means of settling interpersonal disputes resulting from the defense of honor, person, or property. Both the features of the killings themselves and the historical-cultural complex within which they occurred indicate that such was indeed the case. Although not all residents of the State Line country took part in or even condoned the violence that characterized the area, this subregional pocket of culture tolerated violence within well-established limits as a method of maintaining social order.

This case study of homicidal behavior in one small area of the South raises the broader question of southern homicides in general. The high incidence of homicide in the 12 southern states has long been the subject of investigation by social scientists. They point to statistics indicating that the composite homicide rate for the Census South, including both whites and blacks, stands high above that of other census regions in the number of homicide deaths per 100,000 inhabitants, and that such has historically been the case. For instance, the homicide rate in the South for 1920 and 1925 was more than two and a half times the rate for the nation as a whole[22] (see table 5).[23] By 1940, however, the South's 18 homicide deaths per 100,000 persons was only 4 above the national average. The regional gap in the homicide rate has remained about the same from that time to the present, although the total numbers for all parts of the country have gradually, if erratically, decreased from year to year. The figure for the southern states dropped to 11 in 1970, rose again to 13 in 1975 and 1980, and dropped to 10 in 1983, just two above the national average.[24] While the gap continues to close, the South still leads the rest of the country in this respect.

The continuing scholarly disagreements as to the causes of the high homicide rate in the South have produced a voluminous, if contradictory, body of literature that spans more than a century and shows little signs of diminishing. Raymond Gastil, for instance, has contended that there is a "predisposition to lethal violence in southern regional culture." This trait, he says, developed prior to 1850 and persisted over time as a traditional mode of behavior. The regional culture of violence as described by Gastil includes three key characteristics: the presence within the larger culture of more extensive subcultures of violence and/or a large percentage of the

Homicide Rates per 100,000 Population

Years	State Line	South	United States
1850-59	8		
1860-69	24[a]		
1870-79	8[a]		
1880-89	41		
1890-99	41		
1900-09	49		
1910-19	73		
1920-29	114		
1930-39[b,d]	98	22[c]	6
1940-49[d]	20	18[c]	6
1950-59[d]	10	11[e]	5
1960-69	0	9[f]	5
1970-79	24	12[f]	9

Source: Figures for the South and the United States have been compiled from the FBI's *Uniform Crime Reports*, 1932-79, and Brearley, *Homicide in the United States.*

[a]Civil War–related killings are not included.

[b]No figures for the South and the United States available for 1931-32.

[c]Includes only Alabama, Kentucky, Mississippi, and Tennessee.

[d]Figures for the South and the United States apply only to urban areas through 1957.

[e]Includes also Delaware, Maryland, West Virginia, and Washington, D.C. through 1957.

[f]Includes Alabama, Florida, Georgia, Kentucky, Mississippi, North Carolina, South Carolina, Tennessee, and Virginia.

population involved in violence; lethal violence as a significant subtheme in the region's general culture; and lethal weapons and knowledge of their use as an important part of that culture.[25] While these characteristics seem to be substantiated by my own findings in the State Line country, Gastil overextends his position when he claims that, first, the regional culture that produced the violence was already in place prior to the Civil War and, second, that this undesirable southern trait spread horizontally by diffusion and migration from the South to other parts of the nation.[26] In the State Line country, the local violence induced by guerrilla warfare during and after the Civil War refutes the notion of an earlier development of violent regional traits. And the results of migration from the study area clearly contradict Gastil's argument that former southerners continue to commit murder in the areas outside the South to which they have moved.[27] Neither former State Line residents who moved to Northtown nor their offspring born in that city were involved in homicide and other forms of criminal behavior to any significant degree.[28]

To label the entire South as violent on the basis of evidence that is statistically suspect and lacking in holistic cultural and historical perspective is scientifically indefensible. What I have demonstrated here is that the violence in the State Line country stemmed from a fatal code subscribed to by its residents. Furthermore, that fatal code was the natural outgrowth of particular cultural and historical factors originating in the Civil War era and exacerbated by subsequent developments such as moonshining and sawmilling. What is needed now is a series of case studies like this one to arrive at a fuller understanding of the origins and functions of violence in the American South.

My goal here has been to describe and explain homicidal behavior in the State Line country within the context of the area's social and cultural history. To do so required the help of numerous oral narrators who, collectively, had a message for those of us who grew up elsewhere. The fact that they seldom placed blame on either the killer or the victim but looked instead to the motive as a source of legitimation was reflected in their oral narratives about the violence in their home communities. Translated, the consistent message that emerges from their testimony is this: "This is the way our people used to be, and the way they were is the way we are. We may not agree with some of their actions, nor with some of our own in times past, for that matter. But while we're proud that there are far fewer killings today than earlier, we see no reason to apologize for what took place in the past."

Notes

Introduction

1. Wolfgang and Ferracuti, *The Subculture of Violence.*

2. The writings of both social scientists and humanistic scholars have been of considerable help to me in the formulation of this study. Analysis of contemporary criminal behavior has long been the domain of social scientists, as indicated in the bibliography provided by Friedman and Percival in *The Roots of Justice.* Folklorists who have focused attention on oral accounts of crime and violent behavior include Eleanor Wachs, "The Crime-Victim Narrative within an Urban Context," (Ph.D. diss. Indiana University, 1979), and Richard M. Dorson, *Land of the Millrats* (Cambridge, Mass.: Harvard University Press, 1981), 213-31.

3. Information gathered in this manner has been deposited with the tapes at Western Kentucky University.

4. For thoughts relevant to shielding the identities of persons and places studied, see Hicks, "Informant Anonymity and Scientific Accuracy." Serious scholars interested in any aspect of my data can contact me at Western Kentucky University.

5. Harries, *Crime and Environment,* 47.

6. Bankston and Allen, "Rural Social Areas and Patterns of Homicide," 236.

7. Ibid.

8. Charles Joyner decries a similar propensity among historians who have described the southern institution of slavery without first looking in depth at any particular slave community. See his *Down by the Riverside,* xvi-xvii.

1. In the Beginning

1. Arnow, *Seedtime on the Cumberland,* 35-39, provides an interesting line of reasoning to explain why pioneers preferred to settle in the isolated upland areas.

2. Information about the racetrack was obtained from a published collection of historical writings about [Brake] County, which cannot be further described without identifying the county.

168

Notes to Pages 2-21

3. Information about the Masonic lodge was obtained from the published diary of A.B. Alford, a circuit-riding Methodist minister covering the years 1844 to 1892.

4. Glenn, "Physiographic Influences in the Development of Tennessee," 53.

5. The federal census records for the Bear River Valley lists 33 "colored" people—slaves—in 1850; 61 in 1860. A family of blacks lived near Brownsville at the turn of the century, and one of the women was killed by a white man. There were no black families remaining in the study area in the 1980s.

6. Sauer, *Geography of the Pennyroyal*, 139.

7. Bede, Bedes, Bead, and Beads are pseudonyms for a real family name spelled in four different ways.

8. For a description of virtually identical settlement patterns in the Kentucky mountains, see Schwarzweller, Brown, and Mangalam, *Mountain Families in Transition*, 22.

9. Vann Woodward, *Origins of the New South, 1877-1913* 158, corroborates this claim by stating that gunplay, knifing, and killing in the South were more characteristic of the postwar years than the antebellum period. He attributes the increase in violence to the "March of Progress" in the New South following Reconstruction.

10. Troxwell went on from this event to become the infamous Confederate guerrilla still celebrated in oral tradition for his fiendish acts of bloodletting during the Civil War.

11. Hull, *Memoirs*, I:7.

12. For additional comments on the subject of legislative neglect, see Barron, "A Case for Appalachian Demographic History," 211.

13. William Brownlow, Executive Order, in the Tennessee State Archives, Nashville.

14. A recent local newspaper version of the death of Crokes claimed that he was "hooked to a mule and dragged through the streets of Jessetown, and they shot him to pieces."

15. Bartin Billings and his offspring were both killers and victims in the rather large number of homicidal deaths in which they appear to have been involved across the years. Perhaps the Billings family notoriety began with the incident described here. Bart had a son and a grandson who were killed; a second grandson who killed a man, two others who, between them, were suspected of killing close to 20; and a granddaughter who was stabbed and killed by her lover's wife not long after her own son had shot and killed a man at Brownsville. Bart Billings himself was shot to death while stacking lumber in Buffalo Lick Hollow.

16. I am indebted for some of this information to an article by Robert M. Rennick, which I do not identify here in order to preserve the anonymity of the subject.

17. Two brief but informative treatments of moonshining are Holmes, "Moonshining and Collective Violence," and Williams, "Moonshining in the Mountains."

18. Bankston and Allen, "Rural Social Areas and Patterns of Homicide," 232.

19. Cash, *Mind of the South*, 123, makes a similar comment about the South as a whole.

2. The Self-Sufficient Years

1. The social changes brought about by the introduction of commercial lumbering operations did not result in the violent confrontations between labor and management that were witnessed farther east in the Appalachians. For a statement about such activities, see McKinney, "Industrialization and Violence in Appalachia in the 1890's."

2. A search of the Owenton County indictment records uncovered one 1914 bootlegging violation by Claxton besides the one issued for the death of Faris in November 1914.

3. The rival whiskey operation was run by members of the Beauchamp family who, between 1865 and 1933, were indicted by the Owenton County Grand Jury on 111 occasions, mainly on whiskey charges.

4. This information was corroborated on November 14, 1984, by a person whose sister was one of Tault Hardcastle's wives.

5. Information on indictments derived from Owenton County Circuit Court, *Order Books, 1865-1977*.

4. Violence between the World Wars

1. That these matters were incentives to violent action is noted in Matthews, *Neighbor and Kin*, 110.

2. Matthews, ibid., 112, describes this social situation as a cause of violence.

3. This information was obtained from the daily diary/log kept by Minnie Washam Lyons of Honey Creek; it is corroborated by Tennessee's vital statistics records.

4. Kentucky State Board of Health, *Directory: Births and Deaths Registered in Kentucky*. The vital statistics of Tennessee record the death on June 28, 1925.

5. A New Generation

1. For a statement regarding this claim, see Gastil, "Homicide and a Regional Culture of Violence," 412.

Conclusion

1. McKinney, "Industrialization and Violence in Appalachia in the 1890s," makes this claim for the Appalachian region as well. See also Ayers, *Vengeance*

and Justice, for a study of the attitudes of nineteenth-century aristocratic southerners toward the official machinery of law and order.

2. Bruce, *Violence and Culture in the Antebellum South*, 7.

3. Wolfgang, *Patterns in Criminal Homicide*.

4. See also Reed, "Below the Smith and Wesson Line," 144.

5. Studies of the effect of alcohol on violent behavior are summarized by Mednick, "Pharmacological and Biochemical Factors in Violence."

6. An editorial in a local newspaper in 1948 decried the area's poor compliance record for reporting deaths, and urged local citizens to report any and all deaths through the proper channels.

7. Brearley, *Homicide in the United States*, 224, 230-31. See also n. 23.

8. Redfield is cited in Gastil, "Homicide and a Regional Culture of Violence," 105.

9. Reed, "Below the Smith and Wesson Line," 142.

10. McKinney, "Industrialization and Violence in Appalachia in the 1890's," 136, notes that "a mountain man was judged guilty only when he did not live according to community standards. Even murder could be forgiven if the crime was committed for acceptable reasons."

11. Brown, "Southern Violence," 225-30, spoke directly to this point when he wrote that southerners have a "lawful reverence not so much for the legal statutes as for the Bible and unwritten codes, especially those pertaining to personal honor and to the family. While they frequently acted extralegally, they did not do so, in their manner of viewing it, illegally." A consistent argument in Wyatt-Brown's *Southern Honor* is that southerners were more deeply concerned with personal honor and community sanctions than with all other matters.

12. Vogt, *Modern Homesteaders*, 155-59, describes similar attitudes toward the law in a western homesteading community settled by former southerners. The nature and extent of violence and other forms of lawlessness in the State Line country, and local attitudes toward formal law and external authority, closely parallel those prevalent in England during the seventeenth and eighteenth centuries. Of special interest in this connection are the following exemplary studies in British social history: Brewer and Styles, *An Ungovernable People*, esp. 47-127, 172-249; Hay et al., *Albion's Fatal Tree*, 17-63, 119-253; and Macfarlane, *The Justice and the Mare's Ale*, esp. pp. 17-18, 173-79. I am indebted to John Phillips of the University of California at Riverside for bringing these works to my attention.

13. Cash argues for the presence of a southern characteristic of rugged individualism which, he says, was bred on every backwoods frontier and which perpetuated and accelerated the tendency to southern violence. See Cash, "Of the Frontier the Yankee Made," in his *Mind of the South*, 105-47. Individual responsibility in the State Line country is not directly related to his position, however, as Cash was referring to the individualism that characterized southern planters before the Civil War. Further, there is no evidence in the study area to support the widely held notion that the frontier was the natural producer of rugged individualism (see Bruce, *Violence and Culture in*

the Antebellum South, and Cash, *Mind of the South*) or that "each man was a law unto himself" (see Quinney, *Social Reality of Crime*, 229). The necessity of building communities and social institutions and the cooperative effort needed to do so overrode personal considerations.

Reed also questions the position that the frontier created a disposition for southern violence. He further observed (in "Below the Smith and Wesson Line," 141) that "the origins of a trait cannot explain its persistence over time." See also McGrath, *Gunfighters, Highwaymen, and Vigilantes*, 261-71, for a review of the scholarly literature that focuses on frontier violence. McGrath concluded that more serious study of the subject must be done before we can assess the frontier's real contribution to the violence and lawlessness that plague American society.

14. In spite of the lack of reference to blood kin, it was not uncommon for a narrator to comment on inherited traits that seemed to run in families. Typical remarks along these lines included "I don't know who she got that from," or "That's just exactly how his granddaddy acted," or "He'll kill somebody yet; he's just like his daddy."

15. By identifying the early settlers of the study area as "British" in origin, I am in no way entering into the ethnic argument that correlates violence with Celtic stock in the American South, proposed by McWhiney and Jamieson in their controversial study *Attack and Die*, esp. 170-91; see also pp. 200-201 for a listing of additional writings on the subject of southerners and their Celtic heritage.

Upon request, I will provide serious scholars interested in this matter with a confidential list of real surnames of those persons involved in the homicides described herein.

16. Gastil, "Homicide and a Regional Culture of Violence," 417, and Gastil, *Cultural Regions of the United States*, 105.

17. Lamar, "Historical Relevance and the American West," 66, n. 17, questioned the "glib assertion that our tendency to violence can be attributed to our frontier heritage." He observed that western gunmen and outlaws were often veterans of the Civil War, an event that served as a training ground for lethal behavior. That the Civil War influenced Appalachian violence was noted by McKinney, "Industrialization and Violence," 133-34. For additional citations to sources favoring the Civil War as a causative factor of later violence, see Klotter, "Feuds in Appalachia," 310-12.

18. I am aware that any consideration of violent behavior that looks to cultural isolation and to the lack of organized religion and good schools as possible explanations for its origins represents an unpopular position with some regional revisionists. Nonetheless, I feel that my findings justify this stand on the matter.

19. For similar thoughts, see Miller, "Appalachian Values/American Values. Dick and Jane in the Mountains."

20. Federal Bureau of Investigation, *Uniform Crime Reports*, 1940, p. 61.

21. For support of this position, see Barlow, *Introduction to Criminology*, 118.

22. Brearley, *Homicide in the United States*, 19-20, and Brearley, "Pattern of Violence," 685. The rural homicide rate in the southern states for 1920 and 1925 was 11.44 per 100,000 persons. If, as claimed by Brearley, southern blacks committed seven times as many slayings as whites, that would lower the region's white homicide rate to 1.4. Measured against either figure, the State Line country's homicide rate of 114 per 100,000 persons for those years is staggering.

23. As there was no uniform manner of reporting early homicides, any statistics issued were automatically open to question. The demonstrated unreliability of published figures for the State Line country strongly indicates that the same may have been true elsewhere in rural areas of the Upper South. By further inference, statistics for the nation as a whole were likely deflated prior to the 1940s because of unreported homicides. The fact that my tally for the study area approaches accuracy, whereas other geographical areas are most likely represented by incomplete homicide statistics, creates a totally disproportionate picture when rate comparisons are attempted. If regional and national figures were adjusted to compensate for inadequate certification of the actual causes of deaths, the State Line country would be much closer to the average homicide rates.

State Line homicide statistics used in preparing the chart were derived from local sources described in the introduction to this study. Southern and national figures came from Brearley's *Homicide in the United States* and the FBI's *Uniform Crime Reports*, 1930-79.

24. Statistics for the South and the nation as a whole were gleaned from the FBI's *Uniform Crime Reports* for 1930, 1940, 1950, 1960, 1970, 1975, 1980, and 1983.

25. Gastil, "Homicide and a Regional Culture of Violence," 416.

26. Ibid., 412. Gastil's thesis was called into question by Loftin and Hill, "Regional Subculture and Homicide: An Examination of the Gastil-Hackney Thesis," 714. (Hackney has postulated his own cultural explanation of southern violence by attempting to refute several noncultural explanations for the phenomenon. See his "Southern Violence.")

27. Doerner, on the other hand, feels that there is inadequate evidence in support of the position that former southerners continue to commit homicides in the areas outside the South to which they have moved: see Doerner, "A Regional Analysis of Homicide Rates in the United States," 93.

28. Information regarding arrests of former State Line residents was provided by courtesy of Capt. Barton Duke, Records Division, [Northtown], Indiana, Police Department, March 1985.

Works Consulted

Not included in the following list are U.S. Geological Survey quadrangle maps covering the subject area; U.S. Census records for 1880, 1890, 1900, and 1910 on the four counties in the area; highway maps from the Tennessee and Kentucky Departments of Highways; oil and gas maps from the Kentucky Geological Survey; local court records contained in the Kentucky State Archives, Frankfort, and the Tennessee State Library and Archives, Nashville; local courthouse and newspaper files; and other titles containing specific references to places within the study area.

Altman, Irwin. *The Environment and Social Behavior: Privacy, Personal Space, Territory, Crowding.* Monterey, Calif.: Brooks/Cole Publishing, 1975.

Altman, Irwin, and Martin Chemers. *Culture and Environment.* Monterey, Calif.: Brooks/Cole Publishing, 1980.

Arnow, Harriette S. *Seedtime on the Cumberland.* New York: Macmillan, 1960; rpt., Lexington: Univ. Press of Kentucky, 1983.

Ayers, Edward L. *Vengeance and Justice: Crime and Punishment in the 19th-Century American South.* New York: Oxford Univ. Press, 1984.

Bankston, William B., and H. David Allen. "Rural Social Areas and Patterns of Homicide: An Analysis of Lethal Violence in Louisiana." *Rural Sociology* 45 (1980): 223-27.

Barlow, Hugh D. *Introduction to Criminology.* 2d ed. Boston: Little, Brown, 1981.

Barron, Hal Seth. "A Case for Appalachian Demographic History." *Appalachian Journal* 4 (1977): 208-15.

Billings, Dwight. "Culture and Poverty in Appalachia: A Theoretical Discussion and Empirical Analysis." *Social Forces* 53 (1974): 315-23.

Bodenhamer, David J. "Law and Disorder on the Early Frontier: Marion County, Indiana, 1823-1859." *Western Historical Quarterly* 10 (1979): 323-36.

Brazil, John R. "Murder Trials, Murder, and Twenties America." *American Quarterly* 33 (1981): 163-84.

Brearley, H.C. *Homicide in the United States.* Chapel Hill: Univ. of North Carolina Press, 1932.

———. "The Pattern of Violence." In *Culture of the South,* ed. W.T. Couch. Chapel Hill: Univ. of North Carolina Press, 1934.

Brewer, John, and John Styles, eds. *An Ungovernable People: The English and Their Law in the Seventeenth and Eighteenth Centuries.* New Brunswick, N.J.: Rutgers Univ. Press, 1980.

Brown, Richard M. "Southern Violence—Regional Problem or National Nemesis? Legal Attitudes toward Southern Homicide in Historical Perspective." *Vanderbilt Law Review* 32 (1979): 225-50.

———. *Strain of Violence: Historical Studies of American Violence and Vigilantism.* New York: Oxford Univ. Press, 1975.

Bruce, Dickson D., Jr. *Violence and Culture in the Antebellum South.* Austin: Univ. of Texas Press, 1979.

Cash, Wilbur J. *The Mind of the South.* New York: Knopf, 1941; rpt., Vintage Books, 1969.

Chapman, Maristan. "The Mountain Man: An Unbiased View of Our Southern Highlanders." *Century Magazine* 117 (Feb. 1929): 505-11.

Clark, Thomas D. *The Rampaging Frontier.* Indianapolis, Ind.: Bobbs-Merrill, 1939.

Couch, William T., ed. *Culture in the South.* Chapel Hill: Univ. of North Carolina Press, 1934.

Davis, D.H. "The Changing Role of the Kentucky Mountains and the Passing of the Kentucky Mountaineer." *Journal of Geography* 24 (1925): 41-52.

———. "A Study of the Succession of Human Activities in the Kentucky Mountains." *Journal of Geography* 29 (1930): 85-100.

Doerner, William G. "The Index of Southernness Revisited." *Criminology: An Interdisciplinary Journal* 16 (1978): 47-56.

———. "A Regional Analysis of Homicide Rates in the United States." *Criminology: An Interdisciplinary Journal* 13 (1975): 90-101.

Dorson, Richard M. *Land of the Millrats*. Cambridge, Mass.: Harvard Univ. Press, 1981.

Federal Bureau of Investigation. *Uniform Crime Reports*. Washington, D.C.: Government Printing Office, 1930-79.

Ferdinard, Theodore N. "The Offense Patterns and Family Structures of Urban, Village, and Rural Deliquency." *Journal of Criminal Law, Criminology, and Police Science* 55 (1964): 86-93.

Fetterman, John. *Stinking Creek*. New York: Dutton, 1967.

Fisher, Steve, and Jim Foster. "Models for Furthering Revolutionary Praxis in Appalachia." *Appalachian Journal* 6 (1979): 171-96.

Ford, Thomas, ed. *The Southern Appalachian Region: A Survey.* Lexington: Univ. Press of Kentucky, 1962.

Franklin, John H. *The Militant South: 1800-1861*. Cambridge, Mass.: Harvard Univ. Press, 1956.

Friedman, Lawrence M., and Robert V. Percival. *The Roots of Justice: Crime and Punishment in Alameda County, California, 1870-1910*. Chapel Hill: Univ. of North Carolina Press, 1981.

Galle, Omer R., Walter R. Gove, and J. Miller McPherson. "Population Density and Pathology: What Are the Relations for Man?" *Science* 176 (April 7, 1972): 23-30.

Gastil, Raymond D. "Comments." *Criminology: An Interdisciplinary Journal* 16 (1978): 60-66.

———. *Cultural Regions of the United States*. Seattle: Univ. of Washington Press, 1975.

———. "Homicide and a Regional Culture of Violence." *American Sociological Review* 36 (1971): 412-27.

Glenn, L.C. "Physiographic Influences in the Development of Tennessee." *Resources of Tennessee* 5 (April 1915): 53.

Hackney, Sheldon. "Southern Violence." *American Historical Review* 74 (1969): 909-10.

Harries, Keith D. *Crime and the Environment*. Springfield, Ill.: Charles C. Thomas, 1980.

Hay, Douglas, et al. *Albion's Fatal Tree: Crime and Society in Eighteenth-Century England*. New York: Pantheon Books, 1975.

Hicks, George L. "Informant Anonymity and Scientific Accuracy: The Problem of Pseudonyms." *Human Organization* 36 (1977): 214-20.

Holmes, William F. "Moonshining and Collective Violence: Georgia, 1889-1895." *Journal of American History* 67 (1980): 589-611.

Hull, Cordell. *The Memoirs of Cordell Hull*. 2 vols. New York: Macmillan, 1948.

Ireland, Robert M. *Little Kingdoms: The Counties of Kentucky, 1850-1891*. Lexington: Univ. Press of Kentucky, 1976.

Joyner, Charles. *Down by the Riverside: A South Carolina Slave Community*. Urbana: Univ. of Illinois Press, 1984.

Kentucky State Board of Health. *Directory: Births and Deaths Registered in Kentucky*. Frankfort: State Register, 1911-40.

Klotter, James C. "Feuds in Appalachia: An Overview." *Filson Club Quarterly* 56 (1982): 290-317.

Lamar, Howard R. "Historical Relevance and the American West." *Ventures: Magazine of the Yale Graduate School* 8 (1968): 62-70.

Loftin, Colin, and Robert H. Hill. "Comments." *Criminology: An Interdisciplinary Journal* 16 (1978): 56-59.

———. "Regional Subculture and Homicide: An Examination of the Gastil-Hackney Thesis." *American Sociological Review* 39 (1974): 714-24.

Lundsgaarde, Henry P. *Murder in Space City: A Cultural Analysis of Houston Homicide Patterns*. New York: Oxford Univ. Press, 1977.

MacClintock, S.S. "The Kentucky Mountains and their Feuds." *American Journal of Sociology* 7 (1901): 171-87.

Macfarlane, Alan. *The Justice and the Mare's Ale: Law and Disorder in Seventeenth-Century England*. New York: Cambridge Univ. Press, 1981.

McGrath, Roger D. *Gunfighters, Highwaymen, and Vigilantes.* Berkeley: Univ. of California Press, 1984.

McKinney, Gordon B. "Industrialization and Violence in Appalachia in the 1890's." In *An Appalachian Symposium: Essays Written in Honor of Cratis D. Williams,* ed. J.W. Williamson. Boone, N.C.: Appalachian State Univ. Press, 1977.

McWhiney, Grady, and Perry D. Jamieson. *Attack and Die: Civil War Military Tactics and the Southern Heritage.* University: Univ. of Alabama Press, 1982.

Matthews, Elmora M. *Neighbor and Kin: Life in a Tennessee Ridge Community.* Nashville: Vanderbilt Univ. Press, 1965.

Mednick, Sarnoff A. "Pharmacological and Biochemical Factors in Violence." In *Criminal Violence,* ed. Marvin E. Wolfgang and Neil A. Weiner. Beverly Hills, Calif.: Sage Publications, 1982.

Miller, Jim W. "American Values/Appalachian Values. Culture and Environment: Who They Are and Why They're Like They Are." *Appalachian Heritage* 6 (1978): 30-37.

———. "Appalachian Values/American Values: A Certain Self-Consciousness." *Appalachian Heritage* 6 (1978): 47-54.

———. "Appalachian Values/American Values. Dick and Jane in the Mountains: Reassessing the Role of Schools in the Appalachian Region." *Appalachian Heritage* 7 (1979): 49-57.

Montell, William L. *Don't Go Up Kettle Creek: Verbal Legacy of the Upper Cumberland.* Knoxville: Univ. of Tennessee Press, 1983.

———. *The Saga of Coe Ridge: A Study in Oral History.* Knoxville: Univ. of Tennessee Press, 1970.

Mountain Record, 1930-33. Microfilm. Tennessee State Library and Archives, Nashville.

New Era, 1908-55. Microfilm, Kentucky State Archives, Frankfort.

O'Conner, James F., and Alan Lizotte. "The 'Southern Subculture of Violence' Thesis and Patterns of Gun Ownership." *Social Patterns* 25 (1978): 420-29.

O'Dell, Ruth W. "Moonshine in the Tennessee Mountains." *Tennessee Folklore Society Bulletin* 12 (1946): 1-5.

Olmsted, Frederick L. *A Journey in the Back Country*. New York: Putnam, 1907.

Otto, John S. "Oral Traditional History in the Southern Highlands." *Appalachian Journal* 9 (1981): 20-31.

Owsley, Frank L. "The Pattern of Migration and Settlement on the Southern Frontier." *Journal of Southern History* 11 (1945): 147-76.

Quinney, Richard. *The Social Reality of Crime*. Boston: Little, Brown, 1970.

Redfield, Horace V. *Homicide North and South: Being a Comparative View of Crime against the Person in Several Parts of the United States*. N.p., 1880.

Reed, John S. "Below the Smith and Wesson Line: Southern Violence." In *One South: An Ethnic Approach to Regional Culture*. Baton Rouge: Louisiana State Univ. Press, 1982.

———. "To Live—and Die—in Dixie: A Contribution to the Study of Southern Violence." *Political Science Quarterly* 86 (1971): 429-43.

Sauer, Carl O. *Geography of the Pennyroyal*. Frankfort: Kentucky Geological Society, 1927.

Schwartz, Barry. "The Social Psychology of Privacy." *American Journal of Sociology* 73 (1968): 741-52.

Schwarzweller, Harry, Jesse Brown, and Joseph Mangalam. *Mountain Families in Transition*. Philadelphia: Univ. of Pennsylvania Press, 1971.

Slotkin, Richard. *Regeneration through Violence: The Mythology of the American Frontier, 1600-1860*. Middletown, Conn.: Wesleyan Univ. Press, 1973.

Snodgrass, W.R., Frank D. Hinton, and J.T. Francisco. *The Offices of County Medical Examiner and County Coroner in Tennessee*. Nashville: Office of Local Government, 1980.

Stephenson, John B. *Shiloh: A Mountain Community*. Lexington: Univ. Press of Kentucky, 1968.

Stone, Lawrence. "Interpersonal Violence in English Society, 1300-1980." *Past and Present: A Journal of Historical Studies* 101 (1983): 22-23.

Tapp, Hambleton, and James C. Klotter. *Kentucky: Decades of*

Discord, 1865-1900. Frankfort: Kentucky Historical Society, 1977.

Trout, Allen M. "The Man-Form Apparition of Hat Hollow." Brake County *Recorder*, August 18, 1949; rpt. from the Louisville *Courier-Journal*.

Upper Cumberland Times, 1946-63. Microfilm, Tennessee State Library and Archives, Nashville

Vogt, Evon Z. *Modern Homesteaders: The Life of A Twentieth Century Frontier Community.* Cambridge, Mass.: Belknap Press, 1955.

Wachs, Eleanor. "The Crime-Victim Narrative within an Urban Context." Ph.D. diss. Indiana University, 1979.

Webb, George W. "The Settlement Pattern on the Cumberland Plateau in Tennessee." *Journal of the Tennessee Academy of Science* 35 (1960): 24-30.

Wheeler, Lester R. "A Study of the Remote Mountain People of the Tennessee Valley." *Journal of the Tennessee Academy of Science* 10 (1935): 33-36.

Whitaker, J.R. "Tennessee—Earth Factors in Settlement and Land Use." *Tennessee Historical Quarterly* 5 (1946): 195-211.

Wilhelm, Gene, Jr. "Folk Culture History of the Blue Ridge Mountains." *Appalachian Journal* 2 (1975): 192-222.

_____. "Folk Geography of the Blue Ridge Mountains." *Pioneer America* 11 (1970): 29-40.

_____. "Folk Settlements in the Blue Ridge Mountains." *Appalachian Journal* 5 (1978): 204-45.

Williams, Cratis D. "Moonshining in the Mountains." *North Carolina Folklore* 15 (1967): 11-17.

_____. "The Southern Mountaineer in Fact and Fiction. Dead Time and the Lost Frontier: The Mountaineer as Reported by Travelers." *Appalachian Journal* 3 (1975): 42-61.

Wolfgang, Marvin E. *Patterns in Criminal Homicide.* Philadelphia: Univ. of Pennsylvania Press, 1958.

Wolfgang, Marvin E., and Franco Ferracuti. *The Subculture of Violence: Toward an Integrated Theory in Criminology.* London: Tavistock Publications, 1967.

Woodward, C. Vann. *Origins of the New South, 1877-1913.* Baton Rouge: Louisiana State Univ. Press, 1951.

Wyatt-Brown, Bertram. *Southern Honor: Ethics and Behavior in the Old South.* New York: Oxford Univ. Press, 1982.

Index